MW00323473

THE
GAP

www.amplifypublishing.com

The Gap

For more information, please contact:
Mascot Books
620 Herndon Parkway #320
Herndon, VA 20170
info@mascotbooks.com

Library of Congress Control Number: 2018914766

CPSIA Code: PRFRE0419A
ISBN-13: 978-1-64307-413-9

Printed in Canada

THE

The Little Space Between
What You Know and Don't Know

GAP

DOUGLAS VIGLIOTTI

CONTENTS

AUTHOR'S NOTE

We're living through a particularly interesting time. Modern technology has created a world abundant with information. A world full of content producers eager to guide you. A world with ample ways to distribute that content. A world where information travels faster than ever before. A world that seems to get louder and crazier every day. A world that's confusing yet opportunity rich at the same time.

It's my hope to provide you with some quiet time and clarity, with a touch of inspiration. A little book that will provide direction on learning, growing, and exploring in a noisy world. At the very least, a book that will challenge you to look at the world a bit differently. It's no longer up to me, though. The book is in your hands now.

It all starts with the Gap, and this book will help you close it.

INTRODUCTION

"There's a reason they make chocolate and vanilla, too."

Sturgill Simpson

A woman shutters her business two years after opening it.

A lovestruck man puzzles over why his girlfriend refused his proposal.

A first-generation college graduate wonders if Dad will even attend the ceremony.

All these things seem inexplicable, but they're not mysteries. They're the kind of things that happen to us when we don't know what we don't know. The kind of things that change our lives. And what do all these frustrating moments have in common? They're all effects of the Gap.

The Gap is that little space between what you know and what you don't know. It's the only thing that separates you from what you want to understand about yourself, relationships, business, and life. In short, it's a small thing that means *everything*.

Let's look at a quick example together:

Have you ever heard this saying? "The only things certain

in life are death and taxes." Maybe some variation. It's quite popular. It's often attributed to Benjamin Franklin, from a letter he wrote about the US Constitution in 1789. When you dig deeper, however, you'll find Edward Ward wrote something eerily similar in his 1724 book, *The Dancing Devils*. And even before him, author Christopher Bullock in *The Cobbler of Preston* from 1716.[1] So who originally said it? It certainly wasn't Franklin, as so many people think. Was it Bullock? Maybe—but we'd have to keep digging to know for sure.

Similarly, the Gap will prevent you from fully understanding those friends you desperately want to reconnect with, politicians on the other side of the aisle, and relatives who make you shake your head. The Gap is the reason 33 percent of small businesses fail within two years. The Gap is the reason why half of marriages end in divorce.[2] The Gap is why entire generations don't seem to understand *other* generations.[3] The Gap is our greatest human struggle. It doesn't see black or white. Woman or man. East Coast, Midland, or West Coast. Urban, suburban, or rural. Low, middle, or upper class. The Gap poses an equal threat to every one of us. The Gap closes businesses, ends relationships, and breaks hearts.

So if the stakes are so high, why aren't we all trying to close the Gap every second of every day? Because it's much easier not to. It's easier to abandon the relationship with your "crazy" uncle than it is to try and understand his worldview. It's easier to close the flailing business than to dig deep and try something new. And it's definitely easier to take your current beliefs, fold them up, tuck them in, and box them away.

I'm not suggesting you must learn everything about everything, or even that you can. I'm suggesting you go deep into the Gap to learn something new. A Gap, or Gaps, you want to close. Not merely so you can have an opinion—although you will. The world has enough noise. I want you to be a unique voice that's part of a bigger discussion.

A voice that might suggest US presidents should have a cabinet half represented by the opposing party. Not in fear of what the opposition might *do*. But in curiosity to find out what they could *learn*.

A voice that might challenge the current structure of the US education system. Not to simply be difficult. But because they're confident there's a better model for future generations.

A voice that might discuss gender, race, or wealth inequality. Not to be controversial. And not because we haven't made *any* progress. But because you recognize inequality is an inevitable reality.

The Gap never *really* goes away.

A world of Gap closers would mean a world of open-minded people. To me, that world looks like a beautiful place. That's why I wrote this book. That world matters.

Actually, I'd like to take this opportunity to amend that famous saying: "The only things certain in life are death, taxes, and the Gap." The Gap never *really* goes away. It's constant. Just when you think you're closing the Gap, it seems to extend itself slightly further on the other side. But that's okay. Because the point is in the attempt. The learning is in the process.

Maybe you're left thinking, *the Gap doesn't feel small at all*. It might even feel big and intimidating. But it's the commitment to closing the Gap that makes it small. It's the realization that growth occurs little by little, chunk by chunk, and iteration upon iteration. It's about understanding what you desire is only achievable through small increments. And what you're about to learn are the real barriers that prevent you from closing the Gap. The challenges inside the Gap. These obstacles will begin to resemble opportunities for you to start narrowing the Gaps in your life.

I want you to use this book as a compass. Each chapter will present a concept that will start off feeling like a mountain between you and what you want, and end off feeling more like a stepping stone to help you navigate whatever Gap you're trying to close.

In some chapters, you will encounter a shaded box. Only read that box if you're ready for a "next-level" interpretation of the Gap. It's meant to further your understanding of what you've just read and/or what you're about to read. It might look and feel something like this:

NOISE: *A modern-day epidemic.*

In any commodity business, there's something known as the race-to-the-bottom effect, where one business undercuts the next based solely on price. Vendor A gives the commodity (product or service) to the customer for $100. Vendor B comes in and says they could give the same commodity for $75. Vendor C says $50, and Vendor A comes back a year later to win that business back at $25. Ultimately, it's a race to the bottom and nobody wins. The cutback on price comes at cost to both the customer and the vendor. It stunts innovation in the industry and vendors provide worse service, since they must cut back somewhere (plus, they're angry), and customers are no longer satisfied. The new service no longer meets their expectations.

Right now, the same effect is happening with information. Information has been commoditized. Information is abundant. Everyone's competing for your attention. It gets worse, though: it's happening at the cost of quality. We've enabled a world that rewards quantity over quality. We're valuing more, *not* less. Not only do we *expect* quantity, but all distribution platforms—Facebook, LinkedIn, YouTube, whatever—*reward* the content producer for quantity over quality. The more posts, the more exposure. The more posts, the more relevant. More, more, more. It all feels eerily similar to our quick business lesson: cheaper, cheaper, cheaper. A race to the bottom.

This predicament is beneficial for neither content producers nor consumers. Content producers are spending less time with their ideas and more time pushing to meet consumer expectation and technology design. On the whole, this creates more bad content, otherwise known as *noise*. In the end, you and I end up being both frustrated and confused—notwithstanding the fact *we've* willingly created this world with the demand for "right now," "cheapest," and "fastest" at any cost. It's an effect that is compounding daily to make the world noisier and noisier and noisier.

Assuming you want to narrow some Gap, I'll pose to you a question: Do you value quality or quantity? If you swear "quality," consider this: Are you truly embracing it? Or are you contributing to the *noise*? It's easy to share content without consuming it. It's easy to create content without fact-checking it. It's easy to say we'd spend 50 percent more on local vegetables, or triple the cost to have handmade furniture. Do we, though? Perhaps our first lesson is to merely understand that, to narrow whatever Gap we're trying to narrow, quality must reign supreme.

With these next-level interpretations, I do recommend you read the entire chapter first and then return to them. It's my hope these next-level interpretations will elevate your thinking just a tad.

As a whole, this book should help you quiet that noise. Of course, we should remember that there will never be a point at which you and I know everything there is to know. This will never change. I'm as sure about this as death and taxes. Each new piece of information, development, person, situation, or problem brings *more* information, developments, people, situations, or problems. The possibilities become endless, viewpoints get scattered, and you can start to lose your way.

Unless you recognize the Gap, approach the Gap, and try to close the Gap. That little space between what you know and what you don't know. It's your North Star. It's your eternal compass that points toward being more open-minded. More understanding of other people around you. More willing to learn more about things you don't know, and things you do know.

Let's go now. It's time to learn how to navigate the Gap.

WORLDVIEWS

"We don't see things as they are,
we see things as we are."

Anaïs Nin

On March 2, 2017, at Middlebury College, the conservative political scientist Charles Murray was successfully deplatformed by liberal activists after being invited to speak. He's been accused of scientific racism for his work in the 1994 book *The Bell Curve.*[4] This caught the attention of Sam Harris, a neuroscientist and philosopher, who deemed the combination of the deplatforming incident and Murray's research compelling enough to host him on his podcast *Waking Up.*[5]

Shortly after, *Vox*, a news website, bashed the Harris-Murray interview. Harris felt his name had been slandered. He reached out to Ezra Klein, then editor-in-chief of *Vox*, asking for the article to be removed. Klein declined. Emails were exchanged. A feud began between the two. Klein, a strong advocate for social justice and equality, pitted against Harris, a strong advocate for science and rationality. Both would probably say they shared the other's interests to different degrees.

They finally sat down to debate Murray's work publically.[6] It lasted two hours. A clash of worldviews never appeared so obvious.

Klein repeatedly addressed the social impacts of Murray's findings. Harris would rebut with his insistence on the importance of being able to evaluate data without defaulting to accusatory claims. Klein would then lash back, challenging Murray's conservative history and his interpretation of the IQ data. Harris argued the necessity of being able to discuss polarizing topics in good faith.

For two hours, on and on it went. Nothing was resolved.

Each one's worldview impacted how he received, shared, and responded to this information. One man running Murray's work through his worldview, and the other running the same information through his worldview. The two men, both well respected in their fields, just couldn't seem to get through to each other. Why? Worldviews.

Worldviews are mostly a combination of upbringing, life experiences, and environment. Environment is everything that surrounds you—your circle of friends, the family you hang out with, the places you visit, your career choices, and what you do on a daily basis. Your worldview is a culmination of everything you've ever experienced in your life.

ITERATION: *Your worldview didn't start with you.*

In 1960, two young British musicians became reacquainted with one another, ten years after they'd first met at Maypole Primary School in Dartford. Now teenagers, they bonded over a love of blues and R&B music. A few years later, they released their first single, a cover of Chuck Berry's "Come On." Over the next several years, they'd release a bunch of albums, mostly covering other great musicians like Berry—Muddy Waters, Bo Diddley, Buddy Holly, Bobby Womack—and only sprinkling in songs written by themselves on occasion. It wasn't until 1966 that two of the greatest rock musicians ever, Mick Jagger and Keith Richards, wrote a full album together.[11] Of course, we know the rest of this story. I mean, it's the Rolling freaking Stones. One of the greatest rock bands of all time.

Everything around you has been created by someone, somewhere, at some time. The cell phone you're holding, building you're in right now, television you watch at night, car you drove to work today, and podcasts or music you listen to while you're in that car. Yes, blues music existed long before Jagger and Richards's blues-like interpretation of it birthed the Rolling Stones. Ultimately, we ended up with classics that will last forever. Honestly, what would a world be like with without *Sticky Fingers* or *Exile on Main St.?*

The world is iterative. Almost nothing is new. It's the *lens* that is new. The lens that you, or anybody else, runs

> information through as they receive it. Everything flows
> through that unique lens. This informs our perspectives
> of the world. It helps to form our worldviews.

Here's where things get tricky: No two people on earth have
the same compounded experiences, which makes everyone's
perspective truly unique. This is why the best CEOs leave their
door open to everyone in their company. Ray Dalio, founder of
Bridgewater Associates, built the world's largest hedge fund on
this core idea.[7] A true "idea meritocracy," where the best idea
wins out no matter who conceives it. Dalio surely understands
the power of worldviews.

Why does this matter to the Gap? Well, you shouldn't just
consider literal fact (or opinion) and literal source when you
receive a new piece of information. Consider the source's
worldview. It's a three-dimensional way to evaluate information.
Worldview evaluation is often a missing element. Now we can
see *why* Klein's political journalist background and Harris's
science academia background affect their interpretation of
Murray's work. We could certainly continue to peel back the
onion and go deeper, but I think you get the point. It's not to say
who was right or wrong. You can make that decision. Assessing
for worldviews will help us understand intent, so we can build
bridges and narrow Gaps in our lives.

I consider worldview assessment the most important aspect
in trying to close the Gap. Otherwise you're potentially not
maximizing the usefulness of information. Most people don't

Consider the source's worldview.

consider worldviews. They let paper titles, stereotypes, and literal information rule the roost. In the absence of worldview assessment, certain information might even be rendered completely useless.

Let's say Ray Dalio makes a statement about the economy. It's great to know the statement and that Dalio said it. What's more important? Ray Dalio's worldview. This will help you temporarily see the world as Dalio. Not as you. This will enable you to understand *why* Dalio is saying what he said. Which is vastly more important than *what* he is saying.

All of this is quite obvious in the political structure of the United States. We allow mere titles like "Democrat" and "Republican" to prevent us from approaching—never mind closing—the Gap. We make blasphemous associations based on titles alone. Which is interesting, because those theoretical titles switched their ideologies sometime around Franklin Roosevelt's New Deal.[8] Consider this: Abraham Lincoln, a pillar of American civil rights, was a Republican.[9] The world doesn't place any credence on his political party title. The world has the luxury of knowing Lincoln's worldview. In today's turbulent times, would that mere title of Republican affect how you receive any information Lincoln provided? Think about that. Herein lies the importance of worldview over literal source or literal fact when looking at new information.

Religion in and of itself shows the power of worldviews. With almost 84 percent of the world believing in some type of religion and approximately 4,200 religions, think of all the possible interpretations for any *one* generic piece of information. There are 2.3 billion Christians who see the world through that lens, 1.8 billion Muslims who see the world through their lens, and 1.2 billion who don't believe in religion at all.[10] As you may have concluded already, worldviews aren't always as obvious as what religion you believe in. Nor what side of the aisle you're on.

A clash of worldviews might be our biggest challenge in closing the Gap. It's hard to get outside yourself and truly understand another person's worldview. Especially if it's clashing with your own. But it's too important. Ask yourself: How did this person grow up? What was their environment like? What are some of their life experiences? This is critical to understanding the impact of how, why, what, when, and where people share what information they share. It's the most effective way to interpret new information. If there's only one thing you take away from this book, it should be to look at worldviews. Assess worldviews. Account for worldviews. They tell the more important story.

MATCHING

"The force is strong with this one."

Darth Vader

One Sunday morning, I really wanted a Bloody Mary. I prefer horseradish in mine. I didn't have any, so I went to God—I mean, Google—and typed in "horseradish brand." In 0.4 seconds, I got 5,090,000 results and Google even curated their top ten results, just for me.

We've grown accustomed to Google's performance. How often have you gone to the second page on your Google search? Exactly. You're *actually* more likely to change your search query than to dig past page one.

Later that day, I logged on to Facebook, and wouldn't you know it, I noticed horseradish brands everywhere. Sure, my awareness was up because I'd just been searching for horseradish. But I was also literally seeing horseradish brands everywhere on Facebook. People, brands, and companies install code on their website known as a "tracking pixel." This provides them data that says, "Hey, I see you flirting with me." Then those people, brands, and companies pay other companies like

Facebook or that random blog you love for ad space. It's kind of like that weird stalker at the bar. The more eye contact you make, the creepier they get. In this case, the more searching and clicking you do, the more horseradish seems to follow you around the internet.

All these modern technology algorithms are designed to give you more of what you want, when you want it, and how you want it.

Google can tell you the best restaurant wherever you're currently located, where to get your car fixed, or literally anything else for that matter. Like what brand of horseradish to buy. Facebook needs to ensure you stay *on* Facebook. So they give you more of what you want. Which means the same news articles from the same people and same entities, all with the same worldviews. Democrats reading why Republicans suck. Republicans reading why Democrats suck. And ad after ad after ad from the websites you visit most often. Remember the horseradish.

Amazon's Alexa remembers every song title or anything else you scream at it. All in attempt to give you more of what you want. She will even play music for you later that you *might* enjoy, of course, without you telling her to do so. Spotify does the same, creating playlists you *might* enjoy based on your listening preferences. Uber pairs you with the closest and best drivers.[12] StubHub with the best tickets at the best prices. Tinder links us with only the people who have also agreed, "Ah, you look decent." Swipe right. Everything is now intentionally designed to match what you want, when you want it, and how you want it. We're a society that demands matching.[13] Matching, though, is counterforce on you closing the Gap.

COUNTERFORCE: *Matching is the base of the iceberg*

Counterforce makes closing the Gap hard. Very hard. Counterforce isn't just relegated to matching. It takes many forms. Many of which you'll become acquainted with over the course of this book. It's anything intentionally or unintentionally preventing you from closing the Gap.

Your bosses expect you to drink the company Kool-Aid and follow the company track. Don't ask too many questions, just do. Counterforce. Family is invested in keeping you the same. It's what they know, it's who they grew up with. Counterforce. Friends want you to be the person they had those wild nights with every time you're together. Counterforce. To close the Gap, you'll have to start actively pushing back on counterforce.

Matching is such a strong form of counterforce because you don't even know it's happening while it's happening. It's the base of the iceberg. You can't see it, but it's there. It feels natural. It feels helpful. It feels affirming. But it's real-life trickery. Just like magic, once it has been exposed, it loses its most potent element of attack: surprise.

> Now that counterforce has been exposed, you'll be able to spot it and start pushing back.

Maybe you're wondering, "What happens to all the other opinions, articles, companies, partners, worldviews, and pieces of information?" You know, the stuff you're *not* matched with. The unmatches. A private study reviewed 900 million web pages and found 91 percent get no traffic from Google.[14] So the answer is simple: you don't see them. Unless you start pushing back on counterforce. Unless you're actively looking for other points of view and pieces of information and are open-minded to other possibilities. Unless you're embracing the Gap.

I'm not suggesting matching is *all* bad, nor am I completely advocating against it. I previously wrote about the four main drivers of value in my book *The Salesperson Paradox*.[15] Matching appeals to these four drivers, which are time, ease, status, and money. Matching will save you time, make your life easier, improve or maintain your status, and might even save or earn you money. It will also prevent you from closing the Gap. All these smart companies use matching to give us immense value, provide short-term benefits, and win our attention. Just like Google, who matched us with the ten best horseradish queries.

For navigating the Gap, matching is undeniably dangerous. Matching encourages us to stay the same. It ensures we only engage with people like us, ideas we know, and environments we grew up in. That we read the same news articles from the same news outlets. That we almost never go past page one. It's like the perfect storm trying to prevent us from closing the Gap. Trying to close the Gap in a world of matching is the equivalent of trying to remove sugar from your diet while working in a candy store. Impossible to avoid and deliciously tempting.

Matching encourages us to stay the same.

Perhaps it's time to start asking yourself what's more important: closing the Gap, or short-term benefits? Matching is ferociously fighting to limit your ability to close whatever Gap you're trying to close. Matching is baked into society. It's inevitable, but maybe it's time to start exploring the trade-offs it forces us to make.

UNKNOWN

"Overall, I'm more interested in reading books I
disagree with than books I agree with."

Tyler Cowen

When I was kid, I was afraid of the boogie monster. The
boogie monster used to scare the bejeezus out of me. Each
night, I was so scared that I had to cuddle up to my teddy bear;
his name was Teddy.

The only thing scarier than the boogie monster was the
realization that he lived under my bed. I'd go to sleep every
night worrying about what lurked beneath me. I'd yell out to
my mother. She would burst into my room and let out a sigh
of relief. Now, I can only imagine she was thinking, "You've
got to be kidding me. Again?!" She'd tell me a bedtime story
and I'd fall asleep.

This scenario would come to be symbolic for pretty much
everything I've experienced in the rest of my life. The boogie
monster representing the unknown. Teddy, my mom, and
her bedtime stories representing the known. *The unknown is
uncomfortable. The known is comfortable.*

Of course, the problem with all this is that closing the Gap requires change from the norm. It requires doing something different. It requires seeking out that little bit more. It requires growth. As long as the boogie monster remains unknown, it will continue to scare the daylights out of you. You have to face the boogie monster to find out whether it's real or not.

One day, instead of screaming for my mom, I climbed out of the sheets and looked underneath my bed. And wouldn't you know it: there was no boogie monster. The boogie monster was in my head. I ditched Teddy. Finally, I slept in peace.

You have to face the enemy. Maybe you have a strong allegiance to a political party. This isn't meant to oversimplify what it takes, but it just might be time for you to truly face the enemy. Not from your side of the aisle. From theirs. Go mingle, discuss, read, and discover what their world is like experienced from their shoes. Don't be jaded by past experiences. Look at the reality, not your ideal. Understand their worldviews. Why do certain sticking points matter to them? How did they grow up? What is affecting their perspectives? Why do they believe what they believe? How does all of this affect their lives?

Potentially, you'll reveal the enemy isn't really an enemy at all. They may actually have a lot in common with you. Laugh and cry, just like you. Have children they love, just like you. Bills to pay, just like you. It can be quite enlightening. Maybe the enemy is actually fear. Fear of what you might find out. Fear of looking silly for not knowing what you think

You have to face the enemy.

you should know. Fear of simply not knowing anything at all. Stop now and face it. Look silly—who cares. You might be surprised what you find out. Now you're starting to close the Gap.

LEARN: *An opportunity hidden in plain sight.*

On September 21, 1970, a historic event occurred in America: the Cleveland Browns defeated the New York Jets, 31-21, in front of a crowd of over 85,000.

What made this game so special? It was the birth of iconic Monday Night Football (MNF).

Until then, the National Football League (NFL) always played their games during the day on Sundays. Each and every Sunday, the world stopped while rabid fans rooted on their favorite football team. But on that Monday, everything changed. The NFL forever changed primetime TV programming in America.[16] MNF ended up being a blockbuster event. The ratings killed, and it was a huge success. It is a cash cow the NFL continues to milk up to the present day. As of 2018, ESPN pays the NFL $1.9 billion a year to air MNF.[17] This success was later leveraged into a Sunday *night* game, which NBCUniversal pays $950 million a year for. And a Thursday night game, which 21st Century Fox pays $660 million a year for.[18] Sure, there have been multiple factors that have accounted for the NFL's success. Still though, not bad for what started out as the NFL facing the unknown: an undesirable Monday night time slot, long associated with crappy ratings.

Personally, I don't like MNF. The game starts around 9 p.m. EST. Every night, I go to sleep between 9 p.m. and 10 p.m. I might even suggest it's my enemy. I despise it. I believe every game should be played at 1 p.m. EST or 4:30 p.m. EST on Sundays. Just because I don't like MNF and I don't agree with MNF's intent *doesn't* mean there isn't a lot to learn from MNF. Why has Monday Night Football been so successful? How can I apply those same concepts in my life? Or business?

Perhaps its success comes down to the scarcity factor. It *only* happens on Monday nights. It's the *only* game on television, and it *only* happens once a week. It's your one and *only* shot to watch MNF. Maybe it's the get-them-while-they're-hot factor. Most people are still carrying that football hangover from the weekend. They argued with friends about Sunday's bad calls at the watercooler and lost money gambling, and now they get a chance to do it *one* more time. This all really starts to set in when they begin to consider the reality of the week ahead. The cubicle. Their boss. The commute to work. The errands. The wait until next weekend. Is it possible you can use these principles to close the Gap you're looking to close? Maybe. Maybe not. The point is, enemies can provide insight. Face them.

I can't pretend to know what your life is like or what problems you have, situations you're facing, or Gaps you're trying to close. I don't know you. I know this isn't a book about the NFL or how to perform better in your business. Although it might help you in your business. It's a book encouraging you to be more open-minded. Even to things you might disdain. It's a book that will show you can still learn from those things, and potentially use them to help you close different Gaps in your life. And for the record, I *used* to love Monday Night Football.

Many people object to other people's points of view, ideas, and ways of thought, mainly because they don't *truly* understand them. They think they do, and they just don't agree with them. This scenario is totally possible. It's also possible they could be failing to account for worldviews and counterforce. All the things that clearly affect how we receive and share information. And that clearly affect how we apply what we've learned.

The greatest skill that leads to being able to close the Gap is being able to face the enemy. The power to entertain ideas or beliefs totally separate from your own. After that, you can decide whether or not you accept them. There's still a major benefit, even if you truly don't wholeheartedly agree with the enemy. Through an open mind, you'll learn the enemy's strengths and weaknesses. You can use successful concepts the enemy uses in your own life with *different* intent—*your* intent. At the very least, you might learn how to defeat the enemy.

You never know what will birth inspiration or teach you something valuable. View the world through *that* lens. You'll be amazed at what you might see. Or what you might not see. Just like the boogie monster, what you fear might not be real at all. The unknown isn't that scary, I promise.

GATEKEEPERS

"No one can make you feel inferior
without your consent."

Eleanor Roosevelt

In 1970, *The Tonight Show Starring Johnny Carson* was one of the most popular shows on TV. For a comedian, getting a five-minute spot on Carson's show meant you'd arrived. Not because you were better than everyone else. Just because Carson thought so. Carson helped launch the careers of Jerry Seinfeld, Jim Carrey, Jay Leno, David Letterman, and Garry Shandling. The list goes on and on: Roseanne Barr, Joan Rivers, Ellen DeGeneres, Bill Maher, and Kevin Nealon.[19] The most sought-after moment came when Carson *really* enjoyed your set: he would call you over to the couch. In a 1996 interview, Drew Carey remembered being called over to the couch. He said, "The very next day, I was in show business."[20] Making it to the couch was a rare thing. Comedian Louie Anderson didn't make it during his first appearance, but he recalls getting the next best thing: a curtain call and on-camera handshake.[21] The Showtime comedy-drama

I'm Dying Up Here, about the 1970s LA comedy scene, depicts comics throwing "watch parties" and scrutinizing their fellow comics' *Tonight Show* performances. Of course, the crowd goes wild every time someone "gets the couch."

Being on *The Tonight Show* meant you'd arrived. For the most part, this was true. The limited options to distribute and amplify your comedic talent made *The Tonight Show* the Holy Grail of comedy and Johnny Carson king gatekeeper of comedians everywhere. *Gatekeepers are people you rely on for approval.* Some might argue late-night shows still provide this platform for comedians. Sure, these shows all host comedians on a regular basis, but easier distribution and modern technology have changed everything.

ACCESS: *The floodgates are now open.*

In the late 1950s, TV really started to play a vital role in American culture. During most of the 1960s and '70s, there were three major players in broadcasting: NBC, CBS, and ABC. We didn't even have color broadcasting until around 1964—a development that really helped aid TV's explosion in popularity.[22] But there was a small problem. Since there were so few broadcasting companies, it meant restricted distribution for entertainers. Access to America's most beloved and powerful amplification tool was limited to being at the right place at the right time. And if you were, you might just strike it big. I'm not suggesting luck was the only factor in show business during that time period. I'm suggesting that such limited access to airtime meant that gaining that access was more than likely the critical factor in reaching an audience large enough to strike it big.

It's safe to say access has changed quite a bit over the last fifty years. Nothing has contributed to this more than the shifts we've seen in consumer technology. Technology has been moving *fast* over the last five decades. We went from radio to television to the internet to everything in the palm of your hand. This has made for countless numbers of content platforms. YouTube is a free platform. Facebook is a free platform. Instagram is a free platform. The podcast boom is in full swing. The bottom line is that now we have open distribution and amplification of content. We now have unlimited access.

The whole idea of gatekeepers has been completely flipped on its head. Not in the way you might think, though. I often hear people say gatekeepers don't exist anymore. That there are so many ways to distribute your creative work that we have effectively eliminated gatekeepers. Anyone can start a YouTube channel, podcast, or blog. Distribution channels are plentiful. James Altucher, one of my favorite podcast entertainers, talks about this no-more-gatekeeper concept so often it got me questioning the idea. Then it dawned on me. One person doesn't make up the masses. However, we give that power to people or media outlets both consciously and unconsciously. Power only exists where you grant it. It's something you give with your attention and focus. Be careful. Where you grant power has power over you. They or it can make you powerful or powerless. Where are you giving power today?

Where you grant power has power over you.

We still have gatekeepers. Gatekeepers will *never* go away. The difference between the days of Johnny Carson and now is that we *choose* our gatekeepers. This can be just as restrictive when trying to close the Gap as with any traditional gatekeeper. It's another form of counterforce to push back on as we close the Gaps in our lives. I listen to Altucher all the time. I started to view the world as he does, read the books he recommends, and dig up more information about the guests he interviews. At a surface level, this is great. I've found entertainment that satisfies me. No more boring drives to work. It also means I've allowed Altucher to be a gatekeeper of the information I receive. I've given Altucher power over me. I still listen to Altucher—he's awesome—but I've put myself on an Altucher diet. I have intentionally diversified my listening to get alternate perspectives.

You might be consciously choosing to watch your favorite news channel. To listen to your favorite radio station. To read your favorite blog. It's entertaining. I get it. I do the same thing. You're also unconsciously granting power to gatekeepers. Gatekeepers, filtering your life. Gatekeepers, leading you one way or the other. Gatekeepers, who all have their own gatekeepers, worldviews, and problems.

SPECIALISTS

"The best way to find out if you can trust
somebody is to trust them."

Ernest Hemingway

One surgeon, one anesthesiologist, one nurse, one scrub tech, and one sales representative walk into a room. Where are you? Don't think too hard. Chances are you'd be sleeping anyway. You're in an operating room. I've been the sales representative in that room. Sometimes there's a few other people there as well. Maybe you're in a teaching institution. Then it's possible there would be a surgical resident or fellow training under the surgeon. Let's leave them out of this scenario right now.

The surgeon's job is to make sure the procedure gets done correctly. Everyone in the room is relying on their skill set. They have to perform the actual surgery.

The scrub tech is the only person who can actually assist the surgeon. Both are classified as sterile, which basically means washed up, draped in sterile gowns, and germ-free. They're not allowed to touch anything unsterile until the procedure is complete.

The nurse ensures everything is going smoothly. The patient is comfortable. All the sterile equipment is safely delivered and opened. The proper paperwork is filed throughout the surgery.

The anesthesiologist is there to put the patient to sleep and ensure they remain sleeping soundly throughout the procedure.

The sales representative is there to make sure everyone has a good time. Kidding. They're responsible for specific product and tool knowledge that will be used in the procedure.

Each person is specializing in their role to achieve one primary goal: the best possible outcome for the patient.

I've only accounted for the operating room, but before you, the patient, enter that room, you've likely gone through multiple phases of pre-op preparation. You been in contact with various components, checkpoints, and caregivers at the hospital. After the surgery, you'll deal with post-op treatment both at the hospital, in the recovery unit, and externally, in physical therapy. All these points lead to one primary goal: the best possible outcome for you, the patient.

The surgeon can't perform *all* the tasks needed to get the patient back to health. Even though they're the one getting the Yelp review. They're the one who spent thirteen years learning and training to be a surgeon. Regardless, they still have to rely on specialists. What makes us think we don't have to in our lives? You should be relying on specialists, too. *Specialists are people you rely on for advice.*

CONTRADICTION: *Whaddaya want from me?*

In the late 1960s and early '70s, America was coming off the civil rights movement. Vietnam had reached its tipping point. The counterculture era was in full swing. Technology advancements started making it possible to influence and reach the masses. Musicians and creatives had the *access* to distribute and amplify their messages. Messages that were inspired by the political and social challenges of that time. All of this started to raise many questions in the minds of the American people.

It's no coincidence there was a sharp decline in voter turnout for US presidential elections starting with the 1972 election. From 1828 to 1968, there were thirty-six elections, which averaged a 65.24 percent voter turnout. From 1972 to 2016, there were twelve elections, which averaged a 53.62 percent voter turnout.[24] That's an 11.62 percent decline in voter turnout, or approximately 28.9 million fewer voters. This decline represents a classic case of one person (or group) says one thing, and then another says something different, and we decide, "Screw it. Let's not even vote."

In short, contradictory ideas started making us stumble. This issue has only been magnified with rapid technology advancement. Access unhinged. Distribution methods plentiful. Specialists galore. Opinions everywhere. I guess you can say we're still stumbling. But don't let varying ideas thwart your ideas. As they say in boxing, stick and move, stick and move.

Undoubtedly, specialists are valuable. They've done much of the heavy lifting for you. They've spent considerable time and energy. They've put in the work to get really good at a certain thing. Just so the world can rely on them for that thing. Naturally, this raises the question: What specialists should I be trusting?

If I were you, I'd start small. Nobody should be exempt from a healthy degree of skepticism. Trust specialists, but don't be too trusting. Look at the specialists you're currently trusting every day. The people you rely on for answers, advice, and direction. Do you turn to the sports channel to get the weather? Do you turn to the weather channel to get sports news? Where do you go for your information? Is it the correct specialist for that specific information? Do you turn to Twitter for news? Is this the right specialist? Or maybe just another example of current technology appealing to ease, time, money, or status. Maybe more counterforce by matching. Maybe not. Maybe you're tuned into the right specialist.

Is it possible you're falling victim to the halo effect? You might be assuming correlations that aren't necessarily true.[23] As in, you've put a halo around the specialist. One thing doesn't necessarily make something else true. It's best practice to not assume credibility. If you ask an orthopedic surgeon why your heart races after you do yard work, they're going to tell you to make an appointment with the cardiologist. Just because sources are credible in one specialty doesn't guarantee credibility in another. We make this mistake often with our specialists. Blanket

Trust specialists, but don't be too trusting.

trust in specialists can have an adverse effect. Instead of closing the Gap, you could be widening it.

INTEREST

"What matters isn't what a person has or doesn't have; it is what he or she is afraid of losing."

Nassim Nicholas Taleb

I drink two cups of coffee every morning. I don't know why. Probably caffeine. That would be the easy answer. I think it's actually more just the act of doing it. In any case, I truly do love my coffee. Throughout my day, I sometimes find myself in a conversation about coffee. It could be about a favorite roast—light, medium, or dark. Perhaps a favorite bean—arabica, robusta, or blended. Some people prefer French press, cold brew, or just a shot of espresso. This doesn't even include mixed coffee drinks, like cappuccinos, macchiatos, americanos, or whatever clever drinks Starbucks comes up with next.

One day, I was having a conversation with someone at the gym, and her name was Kaitlin. She told me the *best* coffee was at this small coffee shop down the street. I remember her saying, "Silky, nutty, and flavorful." Naturally, I thought to myself, "I have to check this out." Admittedly, I'm not much of a gym conversationalist. I didn't ask too many more questions, and the conversation changed slightly. Anyway, later that week, I remembered that interaction and pulled into the coffee shop.

A little bell sounded as I walked through the door. The barista picked up her head and said, "Good morning, sir. What would you like?" I told her a small black coffee. Light roast, please. We ended up chatting—you know, all the small talk. She was able to explain differences in the coffee blends quite well. As I was about to walk out, she asked, "Hey, we're kind of tucked away over here. How did you find us?" I said, "You've got a raving customer out there. A woman at the gym named Kaitlin recommended your shop to me." She smirked and said, "Kaitlin isn't just a customer—she's the owner."

Most *everyone* has some form of private interest.

Gatekeepers and specialists often have *private interests*. Sometimes they're explicitly obvious and sometimes not. Either way, understanding the potential impact of private interests on their advice, ideas, and opinions is important for Gap closers. These aren't just worldviews. These are private interests that build equity, make money, and improve their lives. They strongly influence how we share information. It's not that I wouldn't have gone to this coffee shop. Nor was Kaitlin lying to me. It's that when you're trying to close the Gap, you should always be accounting for the influence private interests have on how information is shared and received. Many of the specialists and gatekeepers you trust for advice have private interests. All those news outlets you read, channels you watch, podcasts you listen to, and influencers you follow on social media—most have private interests. Most *everyone* has some form of private interest.

For the number of times we've heard about the good ol' boys club or watched depictions of handshake deals in movies, you'd think we'd be more cognizant of private interests. Nobody is exempt. We've seen it on a local level with the neighborhood coffee shop. This idea also scales to corporations, news outlets, and specialists who influence the way we live. Consider this: the world's richest man, Amazon founder and CEO Jeff Bezos, purchased *The Washington Post* for $250 million in 2013.[25] At the time of writing, Salesforce founder and CEO Marc Benioff has just purchased *Time* magazine.[26] This is not meant to be a shot at Bezos, Benioff, or the well-respected *WaPo* and *Time*. I'm not questioning their integrity or making value judgments. I'm merely providing examples that show private interests exist everywhere. Even at the highest levels, like powerful corporations and national news outlets. Private interest has scalability. The larger the interest, the more susceptible it could be to impacting information. It's a good idea to understand your chosen information channels' private interests.

RISK: *Is it worth it?*

In 2018, Tesla CEO Elon Musk took a hit of a joint during an interview on *The Joe Rogan Experience*. I don't really care what Musk does. Smoke, not smoke. Doesn't matter to me. Given the context, I didn't think it was that big of a deal. To me, the more interesting part was the exchange right before. Rogan goes, "You probably can't [smoke] because of stockholders, right?" Musk responded, "I mean, it's legal, right?" "Totally legal," said Rogan. Musk shrugged, "OK."[28]

This seems to be a common predicament in the minds of specialists and gatekeepers: constantly having to evaluate the effect an action, decision, comment, or content share will have on their private interests. Rogan is a comedian who has baked this type of behavior into his brand. It's much of why his podcast is insanely popular. Musk is an entrepreneur solving some of the world's biggest problems. It's much of why he's one of the world's most powerful people. How many "Musks" would take that hit? How many would conclude it's just not worth it to *their* private interests? How many might conclude it is?

For Rogan, this behavior is largely a benefit. For Musk, a fault. It's probably always worth it for us to consider this risk effect on the actions, comments, and information provided by our gatekeepers and specialists. It's likely affecting what they're willing to do, share, or say.

We often see hip-hop star Kanye West pop up in our news feeds for outrageous behavior ahead of an album release. In 2018, a month before the release of his latest album, *Ye*, he dropped this bomb: "When you hear about slavery for 400 years. For 400 years?! That sounds like a choice. Like, you were there for 400 years and it's all of you all?"[27] Just like everyone else, your initial reaction was the same: *wow*. Kanye knows bad media doesn't matter. Its effect is really the same as good media. It will unite avid fans and get non-fans talking about him. In any case, he's at the top of the headlines. His album was #1 on the *Billboard* charts. His private interests are secure. I temporarily debated including this story here, asking myself, "Does Kanye really need another microphone?" But you're a Gap closer, and you know to evaluate for private interests.

Don't allow the fact that private interests exist to make you jaded. Just account for them in your efforts to close the Gap. What are my specialists' or gatekeepers' private interests? Is this information they're providing beneficial to their private interests? Is this information they're providing counterproductive to their private interests? This could be a big reason specialists or gatekeepers might be unwilling or willing to take more risk. A totally reasonable assumption depending on their situation. Ultimately, it will be up to you to weigh the importance of private interests in any given situation.

BIAS

"But suppose we are nothing more than the sum of
our first, naive, random behaviors. What then?"

Dan Ariely

Let's assume you're moving in to a new apartment. This
apartment has different dimensions than your last one. You
want a new desk and desk lamp. You head to the furniture store.
Upon arrival, you find the perfect lamp. Its retail price is $40.
This kind of sucks. You think, "Expensive for a desk lamp!"
Naturally, you pull out your mobile phone and search it. What
do you know—the lamp is on sale for $20 at the furniture store
twenty minutes away. You think, "Wow, 50 percent discount!"
Would it be safe to assume you'd drive the twenty minutes for
the $20 discount? I would. You get to the other store and run
in to buy the lamp. No time for desk shopping right now. You
have somewhere to be. You're cool with that, though. You just
got a deal.

A few days later, you go back to that same furniture store to
look for your desk. You think, "They had a great sale on desk
lamps, so maybe I'll find a steal on a desk." Upon entry, you

see a beautiful desk made of solid oak. Absolutely gorgeous. You want it. It will go perfectly with your new desk lamp. You look at the price tag and it says $500. "Ah, a bit steep, but I do love it," you think. Reminded of what happened a few days ago, you reach into your pocket, grab your mobile phone, and search for a better deal. You're shocked to see that the other furniture store twenty minutes away has it on sale for $480! You ponder, "$20 savings, or I can just pick it up right now. Hmm." Would it be safe to assume you'd just pick up the desk? I would.

We can clearly see that in either case, your dollar savings are the same. The rational thing would be to make the same decision in both scenarios: either drive for the $20 savings or don't drive for the $20 savings. But this isn't how we behave. A clear example of our innate irrationality and a clue that we're indeed prone to cognitive bias.

The first piece of information served as a point of relativity for every other piece of information to follow. We tend to overvalue the first piece of information we receive. Just like how the first time you encountered $20 savings, you jumped on it. Once you saw it relative to the higher amount of $500, you changed your mind. You experienced diminishing sensitivity. The same thing happens when you listen to a new podcast, watch a new video, or read a new article. You'll base whatever else you consume off that first person you heard talk about that topic. This might even come at the cost or absence of validity. This sounds quite dangerous for our Gap-closing efforts.

Now, let's assume you *agree* with that first specialist, gatekeeper,

We tend to overvalue the first piece of information we receive.

or piece of information. You're about to experience some serious counterforce on Gap closing. This first piece of information now serves as your neutral point of relativity. You're more likely to defend than explore. You're valuing a loss over a gain. You're now more likely to connect the dots confirming that first piece with each new bit of information you come across.

ANCHOR: *A tangible reference point for gatekeepers and specialists.*

For all intents and purposes, and depending on who you are, I'm a specialist or gatekeeper. I wrote about a concept in my book *The Salesperson Paradox* called CRINGE Solutions. It's my iteration on the solutions business owners or salespeople should be providing to customers. It's impossible for me to not consider that concept each time I come across new relevant information. It's not that I can't change my mind, decide I was wrong, or improve my thinking. I'm just constantly comparing new information to that concept. It's my tangible point of reference. It's my anchor.

Thanks to the Nobel Prize–winning work of Daniel Kahneman and Amos Tversky, we know a couple things about how specialists and gatekeepers view their anchors.[30] First, how they learn and share new information becomes relative to these tangible points of reference. These references serve as points of relativity when writing their articles, reporting their news, and championing their ideas. Second, since losses are valued higher than gains, specialists and gatekeepers are very protective of their anchors. It's more likely for them to defend than to explore.

Maybe you're thinking, "Doug, isn't this the same as worldviews?" It can be. The main difference with anchors is that a person has written or spoken on these topics. They have more skin in the game. It's best practice to know these anchors on your quest to close the Gap. What are your specialists' and gatekeepers' tangible points of reference? It might be time to explore the alternatives. At minimum, account for them.

Now, indulge me as I belabor a critical point. Imagine you're at a party. You want to capture a photo of you and your friend Jane. You give the camera to a stranger. They take a photo. You get the camera back. Jane says, "Whoa, great photo!" You go, "Really? Should I post it on Facebook?" Jane snaps back, "Of course, it's great!" You post it. Ten minutes goes by, and you check it: five likes. You think, "Okay, it's only been ten minutes." An hour goes by, you check it, and it's at twelve likes. You wonder, "Is this actually a good picture of me?" Two hours, check it, twenty likes. You do more thinking. This process goes on and on. The number of likes is irrelevant. You believe it's a great photo and now you're looking for anything that will confirm it. You're experiencing confirmation bias.

You're looking to confirm your existing belief. An existing belief that was set by Jane, your unintentional photo gatekeeper.

Me, you, gatekeepers, and specialists alike are *all* experiencing innate cognitive biases that affect the way we communicate, share, and learn new information. Quite honestly, confirmation bias is just the tip of the iceberg. There's over 180 documented and known cognitive biases.[29] As is evident from our furniture example, it would be easy to conclude we're *often* not making decisions in our best interest. Don't panic. It's okay. We all do this. You can battle this bias, though. I'd suggest starting small. Evaluate with scrutiny the first time you come into contact with a new idea or piece of information. How is this impacting everything else you've listened to or read on that particular topic? Did you agree with it? If so, start exploring. It's quite possible you're a victim of your own innate biases.

ENTERTAINMENT

"I would rather entertain and hope that people learned something then educate people and hope they were entertained."

Walt Disney

In 1972, an eighteen-year-old boy left home in New York to enroll at Boston University. He started an on-air comedy show at the campus radio station. It got canceled after its obscene first show, "Godzilla Goes to Harlem." The seeds for future stardom were planted. It was that same bravado, brashness, and provocative nature that would get him booted off the AM/FM airwaves. Fired from Clear Channel. Fined $2.5 million by the Federal Communications Commission.[31] All while making him a star. Howard Stern is one of the most recognizable radio voices of all time.

In 2004, Stern signed a five-year, $100 million contract with SiriusXM Satellite Radio, a paid subscription radio service.[32] At the time, Sirius had about 600,000 subscribers. As of 2015, that number had risen to almost 29 million listeners.[33] Stern is often credited with aiding this rapid growth. Stern's show is clearly designed for entertainment. No debate. He knows successful entertainment benefits from being polarizing. Polarity breeds virality. The more you play on the edges, test the boundaries, and challenge the status quo, the greater your chances of going "viral" or spreading rapidly. In hot states, or extreme states of arousal like shock or anger, you're more likely to share a piece of content you've come across online. You're in a perpetually hot state while listening to Stern, and he knows this.

Polarity breeds virality.

In a 2018 interview with David Letterman, Stern admitted, "I would see it was minute fourteen, and I would just say the most ridiculous things to get you to listen."[34] Stern knew ratings were measured in quarter hours. In other words, assuming he could get you to listen past minute fourteen into minute sixteen, that would skyrocket his show's ratings. He wanted listeners in an even hotter state when it mattered most. He felt pressure to be polarizing. Pressure to entertain you.

PRESSURE: *Can you feel it?*

During an NFL game, teams, on average, score the same amount of points in every one-minute segment. However, in the last minute of the first half, teams score more than double compared to any other minute.[36] Teams perform better under pressure. Pressure gets things done. Pressure ensures we meet deadlines, provide consistency to the world, and hang in when the going gets tough. It drives us to create more, learn more, and grow more. Pressure is real. For me. For you. For everyone.

Howard Stern clearly felt external pressure to generate ratings. In the same interview with Letterman, he said, "The pressure is intense. I remember being at NBC and I remember one of the sales guys would walk up to me and say, 'Howard, today's your report card.' And I'd hear 'report card' and this was the worst thing you could say to me. My report card was coming out. The ratings were coming out. And if I was number 1 in the market, it wasn't like some glorious euphoria. It was, 'Phew. How am I going to do this again?'" A plausible recipe might be: more entertainment, more polarity, more shock, more awe, and more anger. And potentially less validity yet more virality. More counterforce on closing the Gap.

Specialists and gatekeepers are under tremendous pressure. Pressure to give their loyal following more of what they want. The loyal following that makes them feel alive. The loyal following that put them on the map. Pressure to perform. Maintain an audience. Brand consistency. Private-interest pressure. Pressure to sell books, fill seats at the concert hall, and ensure advertisers continue advertising on their podcast. Pressure bound by money. All just pushing specialists and gatekeepers more toward entertainment than education.

Typically, there's much ambiguity between entertainment and education. There's definitely a gray area. Confusing the two is likely. Most media programs have elements of both entertainment and education. The rise of podcasts, YouTube, and social media platforms serving as free content distributors has made this gray area even murkier. This means the halo effect might be nudging you again. Are you assuming credibility? Even when the show's clear intent is entertainment? Think about it. Even in the case of Howard Stern, the highest degree of entertainment possible, you're still likely to hear someone haphazardly back up a statement with, "Uh, I don't know. I heard it on Stern this morning?" As Jonah Berger, a professor at the Wharton School of UPenn, has suggested, "Information travels under the guise of what seems like idle chatter."[35]

A key question for Gap closers should be: Is the primary goal of this specialist or gatekeeper to educate or to entertain us? I realize most offer a combination. A little education, a little entertainment. But is their primary goal designed

Is the primary goal of this specialist or gatekeeper to educate or to entertain us?

more for entertainment or education? Is it designed *more* to please you or help you? This doesn't mean you *can't* get entertained by things designed to educate you or educated by things designed to entertain you. This quick analysis just might reveal an indicator that would impact the way *you* receive, share, and explore information. Some things might quickly seem more or less relevant. At the very least, they might annoy you less.

INTELLIGENCE

"The difficulty lies not so much in developing new ideas as in escaping from old ones."

John Maynard Keynes

It's quite likely you've spent a considerable amount of time on one particular subject matter. Maybe you're a small business owner, math teacher, attorney, or salesperson. Maybe you're in the food, healthcare, or education industry. Possibly you're a creative, like a photographer, writer, or musician. You're probably a specialist yourself.

In many cases, specialists just like you have spent years studying a specific subject. Ultimately enabling you to obtain a vast amount of knowledge in one particular area of study. Through both actual experience or research. At first glance, being extremely intelligent in a specific subject matter seems great. It is. I would urge anyone to turn to you for advice. But true intelligence doesn't come without its challenges. It's the Gap we experience once we actually know a considerable amount about a specific topic. It's the Gap we face in our areas of specialty.

The curse of knowledge starts to emerge.[37] The more you know about a particular subject matter, the harder it gets to communicate that knowledge. Think of it like this: everyone starts at baseline or zero, and for every year you study or experience a specific subject matter, you move up one "knowledge point" on the scale. Once you get to level ten or even higher, imagine how hard it becomes to communicate with people at the baseline. Extremely hard. Specialists just like you experience this a great deal.

I know this from firsthand experience. The consulting work I've done with business owners has often boiled down to this very topic. I help true experts communicate to the world what it is that they do. The trick is doing it in a way the world wants. A way the world is able to understand it, use it, and share it. Often doing this act alone significantly improves results. Why? Before, they were communicating at level ten to a customer base who is at zero. If they don't understand you, then how can they buy from you? In my opinion, lack of clarity costs businesses more sales than all other problems combined. This manifests internally as low confidence, discomfort, and fear. Externally, it confuses the customer. It exploits you. How often do you purchase products or services that confuse you? You don't even see them. You only recognize what's super clear to *you*. That's the point. Maybe you have bought an item you didn't understand. You were probably disappointed. When trying to close the Gap, it's important to honestly assess the intelligence level of your specialist versus your current intelligence level in

The more you know about a particular subject matter, the harder it gets to communicate that knowledge.

that particular subject matter. This should improve how you receive, share, and obtain different information, advice, and opinions. It will also help you to defer when necessary. It's about honest assessment. It's all about clarity.

QUESTIONS: *They're the answer.*

In a 2017 study on children, researchers found that kids ask, on average, seventy-three questions a day.[39] I always wonder, "Why do we stop asking?"

Questions are the fuel of continuous learning. It's only normal to start getting complacent, though. You have a career, children, and bills. You have neighbors to keep up with, presents to buy for the holidays, and a boss to make happy. And don't forget the kids' college fund. It's easy to think, "What's the point of changing anything now?" A pressure that seems to only get heavier once you perceive yourself as intelligent: "What's the point of asking more questions? After all, I'm already smart and successful." I guess you can say we willingly stop becoming more intelligent. It makes sense.

Our willingness to stagnate our knowledge level and stop asking questions is intuitive when you consider the lack of incentive. Plus, it's more comfortable. We can't find a good enough reason to learn more and press us to be uncomfortable. So I'll do my best to provide one right now: a lack of commitment to continuous learning will widen whatever Gap you're trying to close. It's a considerably dangerous form of counterforce.

Please, at all costs, *never* stop asking questions.

I want to propose to you another challenge that intelligence brings to the Gap. The more you know about something, the less likely you are to seek out differing opinions. I know you might take me head on with this claim. But you've become a specialist in your own right. Ego will start to nag you, "Stay here, where it's familiar and safe." Think about your reference points, worldviews, audience, private interests, and innate biases. You have a lot of "pressure" to defend your point of view. Confirmation bias really starts to rear its head. Plus, you want to stay where you are, because it makes you happy. It's more comfortable. After all, the great unknown is scary. For me, it doesn't seem unreasonable to assume that the more you know, the more likely you are to anchor on your existing beliefs and to defend your position. Open your mind and explore. You're too smart for your own good.

I'm not suggesting you make radical changes. I'm asking you to become a continuous learner in your chosen specialty and any other Gap you want to close. Mainly because I know you can. Any physiological excuse is wearing, because whether you're sixteen or sixty, it doesn't matter. Your brain has the ability to rewire itself and create new neural pathways at *any* age.[38] Sure, you might have to face the enemy and entertain challenging ideas. You'll have to learn more about differing opinions. You'll probably have to investigate adjacent and nonadjacent industries. All while maintaining a belief that inspiration can stem from anywhere. Because it can. This is what will provide you the insight and encouragement to start narrowing the Gap.

LUMPING

"Don't criticize what you can't understand."

Bob Dylan

In June 1971, President Richard Nixon made a formal declaration, citing drugs as public enemy number one. He declared war on drugs. America's drug problem got worse and worse into the 1980s. In 1984, First Lady Nancy Reagan launched the "Just Say No" campaign.[40] One of the most memorable campaigns in American history. A huge part of the campaign's effort was to flood America with anti-drug ads specifically targeted at teens. The core message was simple: when presented with the option to buy or do drugs, "Just Say No." The intent was great. Spot on. Did the ads work, though?

Robert Hornik, a communications professor at UPenn, evaluated thousands of teens aged 12.5 to 18 years old who saw the anti-drug ads against whether they ever smoked marijuana after seeing the ads.[41] In the end, he concluded the ads were mostly ineffective. His colleague, Jonah Berger, thought a good explanation for this might be that the ads publicized drugs.[42] This actually made kids *want* to try drugs. This feels eerily similar to the idea we discussed earlier with Kanye West—all media is good media, and media can have adverse effects. However, I might suggest another reason why the ads were ineffective.

For our purposes, "Just Say No" violates a major rule of trying to close the Gap. "Just Say No" lumps all drugs together. Wait—isn't that a good thing? When trying to close the Gap, lumping is a massive pitfall. More times than not, lumping will cause an adverse effect. Lumping is a universal problem. We see lumping everywhere.

I really enjoy Riesling. I'm not alone—wine aficionados really like Riesling as well. I'm not an expert, but I can taste why. It's versatile. They applaud it for its ability to take to the terroir and growing conditions better than most other grape varietals. For me, done well, riesling is crisp, dry, and delicious. Which is why I really like French Riesling from the Alsace region, German *trocken* Riesling, and Austrian Riesling. In the US, Finger Lakes or Willamette Valley might offer you a similar style. I offer Riesling to people from time to time. I usually get the same response: "Ah, Riesling. So sweet, how do you drink that stuff?" They're lumping. For them, all Riesling *must* taste like the $5 bottle they drank in college. The one easily confused for grape juice. I can't really blame them for thinking that. It's their worldview. Many default to an even bigger lumped category: "Ah, I don't like white wine." That's a big proclamation. It's sad, though. They're falling victim to lumping. They're potentially missing something special.

Are you lumping people, ideas, and concepts into bigger categories?

Lumping is a big problem for Gap closers. You often miss all the nuances that make something special. You miss the beauty. You miss the differentiation. You miss the details. You miss the genius. You miss the influence. This raises a big question on your Gap closing journey: Are you lumping people, ideas, and concepts into bigger categories? What are your big categories? Where do you draw the line? You're potentially missing difference makers, sources of inspiration, and unique applications for your life. My editor often reminds me, "Doug, specificity leads to universality." She'll urge me to be more specific. Why? If you want something to reach or move people, you have to be more precise. You have to get to the essence. You have to get clear.

Lumping occurs most often when we don't understand something. It's easier to box it up into a broad category for which we have some comprehension. Think about the category "drugs." A little broad, no? There are clearly all kinds of drugs. Different types, usages, and dosages. Some are prescription. Some are over-the-counter. Some are compounded chemicals. Some come from the ground. Some are legal. Some are illegal. Michael Pollan, a professor at UC Berkeley, is leading the charge to showcase research that suggests positive usage for psychedelics.[43] For a long time, drugs like LSD and psilocybin (magic mushrooms) were under tremendous scrutiny. Now, modern research indicates that used in the right dosage, these drugs could have health benefits for people dealing with cancer, terminal illnesses, depression, and addiction. I'm not advocating you take drugs. I'm advocating for you not to lump. Otherwise, you'll completely miss information that might help you close the Gap. That can happen with drugs or anything else. It's probably best to ask yourself, "Where are my categories too big right now?"

OUTCOMES

"What is to give light must endure burning."

Viktor Frankl

Every day, hundreds of thousands of kids play basketball. With each basket, they envision that legendary winning-shot narrative: *It's down to the wire with three seconds left on the clock. Can he do it?* Different kids, same story. I know I imagined this moment of glory countless times. Even when I wasn't outside in the driveway or down at the park. I'd still imagine it with every crumpled-up paper tossed toward the trash can. Heck, I still do it today. Only very few ever get to actually experience this feeling. Never mind experiencing it at the highest level, playing in the NBA. Even fewer get their number called at the end of the game to take that shot.

For one boy, these imaginary shots turned into a twenty-year career: eighteen-time all-star, five-time NBA champion, two as MVP, and third all-time on the points-scored list.[44] Kobe Bryant is widely considered one of the greatest basketball players to ever grace the court. He often had his name called to take that buzzer beater. What made Kobe, Kobe?

In 2016, he was interviewed at a TEDx event in Shanghai. He had many words of wisdom. Although I don't think any were as important in providing an answer to the question above as the ones below. When asked why he wakes up to train at 4 a.m., this was Kobe's response:

It just makes sense...If your job is to be the best basketball player that you can be, right? To do that you have to practice, you have to train, right? You want to train as often as you can, as much as you can. So, if you get up at 10 a.m. and train at 11, right, okay, 12. Train for two hours, so let's say 12 to 2. You have to let your body recover, so you eat, you recover, whatever. You start training at 6, 6 to 8, and now you go home, you shower, you eat dinner, you go to bed, you wake up and do it again, right? Those are two sessions.

Now, imagine you wake up at 3, train at 4, go 4 to 6. Come home, breakfast, relax, blah, blah. Now you're back at it again 9 to 11, relax, whatever, and now you're back at it again 2 to 4, and now you're back at it again 7 to 9. Look at how much more training I've done by simply starting at 4 a.m. So, you do that. And as the years go on, the separation that you have with your competitors and peers just grows larger, larger, larger, and larger, and larger. By year five or six, it doesn't matter what kind of work they're doing in the summer. They're never going to catch up. They're five years behind.[45]

You might be thinking, *I get it—Kobe had an amazing work ethic.* But it goes deeper. Kobe didn't just work harder. He knew his intended outcome but focused only on the process. Kobe's first two lines above are evidence enough of that. He immediately associates being the best basketball player to practice and training. In other words, he just assumes you know that process is what matters most. In late 2015, Kobe wrote a retirement letter for *The Players' Tribune* titled "Dear Basketball":

> As a six-year-old boy
> Deeply in love with you
> I never saw the end of the tunnel.
> I only saw myself
> running out of one.[46]

It was that quote that revealed to me Kobe knew there would never be a true outcome. He values process over outcome. Kobe knew this process would ultimately be his life.

It's hard to adopt this mindset due to what I call the Outcome Fallacy: a societal belief that outcomes are more important than processes.[47] It's the idea that if you can just achieve that one outcome, then everything else will be better. Logically, we know the Outcome Fallacy is just that—a fallacy. We spend 99 percent of our time on earth living the process, not the outcome. No matter what we do, no outcome in the world could replace the fact that we go back to the process tomorrow. You close a big sale. Back to work. The movie premieres. Back to acting. You win the

We spend 99 percent of our time on earth living the process, not the outcome.

game. Back to practice. You don't *have* to do any of those things again, but you'll certainly be doing some *other* process instead. Different process, same process, doesn't matter, there's always a process. Whether you're trying to be the best basketball player, best father, or best teacher. We all fall victim to the Outcome Fallacy.

There are so many things that condition us to believe in the Outcome Fallacy. Our education system focuses on grades rather than learning. Our athletic coaches champion winning over improving. Our bosses scream, "We need more sales!" When they should be saying, "What can we do differently now that we know this?" Our friends remind us, "Live for today. Tomorrow's not guaranteed." Sure, that's true *one* day, but with life expectancy at approximately seventy-nine years, it's also not true approximately 28,834 other days.

Kobe knew it was the compound effect, session after session, year after year, that would provide him the edge he was looking for. You're likely not a professional basketball player, but you *are* playing at a high level. It's your one life. Maybe you're not taking that game-winning shot, but you definitely have pressure to perform. It's placing that same high value on the process of closing the Gap that will matter most to achieving whatever you're looking to achieve. Best mom, best teacher, best doctor, best entrepreneur, doesn't matter. Focus on the process.

Focusing on outcomes means you're competing against the world. Focusing on processes means you're competing against yourself. And I'd take that bet.

RANDOMNESS

"No matter what decision you make there's always more possible futures than the one that will actually happen."

Annie Duke

Most people don't trust their weatherman. When he says, "Today looks like a 30 percent chance of rain." They think, "Just tell me, do I need an umbrella or not?!"

Maybe you've heard of the butterfly effect, a derivative of chaos theory that stems from the notion that a butterfly flapping its wings in South America can affect the weather in Connecticut. In theory, it should teach us to expect the unexpected.[48] It should teach us that randomness is a massive part of everyday life. I know—it's not what you want to hear. But this is why the weatherman uses percentages. I'm no meteorologist, but I don't need to convince you of this fact— random events happen quite often.

Randomness brings with it real problems. Randomness can trick you. Randomness *will* trick you. There is an infinite number of variables that affect any one outcome. Many outcomes you see are not products of process. They're products of randomness. I'm not suggesting your life or anything that happens during it is out of your control. I'm suggesting you should always be assessing for randomness. That is, if you're looking to close the Gap.

The weatherman is looking at decades of data, charts, and trends. He combines this historical data with current conditions, and then he's able to give you a weather prediction. Think about what he's saying—"Approximately one out of every three days, it will rain." Should you *really* be that pissed if it rains? That doesn't seem very unlikely. Maybe now you'll have some more empathy for the weatherman. Probably not. That's okay. Just keep an umbrella in your car.

The key questions are now obvious. Are you viewing outcomes in a narrow or broad frame? Are you looking at individual outcomes or many outcomes over time? Are you looking at the entire picture? The weatherman is looking at the entire picture to close the Gap. The entire picture is where you'll see data, charts, and trends. The entire picture tells a better story. I'd suggest you also look at it. The entire picture will help you account for randomness.

Wait—but why *must* we account for randomness?

MODELING: *Your #1 tactic to close the gap.*

In 1958, President Dwight Eisenhower founded NASA. Without NASA, there would be no Netflix. Wait, what? Yes, you heard me. Okay, here we go—NASA

Are you looking at the entire picture?

launched Apollo 13, Universal Pictures released the motion picture *Apollo 13* in 1995, Reed Hastings rented a DVD version of *Apollo 13*, he misplaced it for six months, it resulted in a $40 late fee, so he wondered how to make sure this didn't happen to other people. In 1997, Reed Hastings founded Netflix. A completely random set of events linked together to birth Netflix.[50]

On the surface, this process can't be replicated. It's completely random. Unless, let's say, you're trying to close the Gap on starting a business or launching an initiative. This anecdote might indicate you should start looking at relevant problems in your life. You might begin to consider whether people are experiencing the same problems as you. Then you'd start thinking about how to solve those problems. Now you're modeling.

Modeling is copying. Not plagiarizing. Not stealing. Just using information, styles, strategies, and concepts from successful outcomes. Heck, I advocate people to model all the time. It's one of the most effective ways to close the Gap on whatever you're trying to do. You're most likely modeling in your life already and don't even realize it. Maybe you do. Naturally, things start to get trickier when you try to model isolated and anecdotal outcomes. That doesn't mean you absolutely shouldn't. It just means you should scrutinize what you're modeling. It will give you a more accurate model to guide *your* decisions and design *your* process.

I'm not discrediting outcomes like winning a million dollars, picking the right stock, making a huge sale, or becoming an overnight celebrity. After all, they're tangible. They're real. They happen. But using isolated outcomes to model only makes accounting for randomness more necessary. Ask yourself, "Is this outcome more a result of process or randomness?" Wouldn't you value any outcome differently depending on the degree of process versus the degree of randomness? Not better or worse. Just more model-able. I would. You can't model randomness. You *can* model process.

The rise of the internet has brought with it real challenges when it comes to randomness. We live in a world with unbridled access to distributing your information, skills, and thoughts. You have a lot of choices on who and what you model. This also means more lucky charlatans are around to trick you with their random outcomes. A true and real pitfall on your Gap-closing efforts. Outcomes are not always what they seem. When you look at them anecdotally, they offer very limited information. But when you treat outcomes like the weatherman, each one seems to be less and less important. You're looking at the entire picture. You're accounting for randomness.

The only way to make sense of all this randomness is to look at things in probabilities, potentialities, and percentages.[49] That's why the weatherman tells you there's a 30 percent chance of rain rather than giving a solid yes or no. He's accounting for randomness.

Are you? With all that being said, is it possible you're giving too much credit or blame to one particular specialist or gatekeeper? Is it possible the guy with the Ferrari on TV just got lucky? Is it possible you're being tricked by randomness? Maybe you should trust the weatherman. He isn't a charlatan trying to trick you with a random outcome. He's a specialist using modeling to close the Gap.

CERTAINTY

"Forty seconds? But I want it now."

Homer Simpson

In 1972, Jerome Kagan, a pioneer in developmental psychology, reached an interesting conclusion.[51] Kagan found it is our desire to resolve uncertainty that sits at the foundation of what motivates our behavior. This "uncertainty resolution" really seems to impact the way we think and act.[52]

Over twenty years later, two psychologists named Arie Kruglanski and Donna Webster found a way to measure this need for "cognitive closure."[53] Our need to fill that void of uncertainty. Their scale is appropriately titled "Need for Closure," or NFC.[54] Kruglanski and Webster found that NFC has a couple interesting side effects. First, it heightens under stress, periods of fatigue, time pressure, and peaks during emergencies. Second, cognitive closure has a "seize and freeze" effect on behavior—we have an immediate urge to satisfy our uncertainty, followed by a prolonged period of protecting that closure. It's often been labeled "motivated closed-mindedness."[55] A phenomenon that serves as a rather obvious foe for Gap closers.

I'm going to propose a quick thought experiment. I want you to consider a few questions:

> Why do you buy from companies that present you with guarantees, free trial periods, case studies, and testimonials?
>
> Why won't you leave your 9-to-5 for that entrepreneurial endeavor?
>
> Why do you choose to stay in that crappy relationship?
>
> Why do you choose unhappiness over uncertainty, time after time?

You might have guessed it. We crave certainty. We want certainty in our purchases, our jobs, our relationships, and our lives. *Most* concerning, though: We want certainty against our best interests. We also crave certainty with advice and from news sources. Which is why we'll listen to anecdotal evidence and charlatans despite rampant clues of randomness. Forget validity, accuracy, or credibility. The more certain, the more believable.

This is probably our best explanation for US social media users relying more and more on social media for their news. Social media is quick and easy. A combination of matching and desire for certainty makes for a dangerously seductive counterforce on social media users trying to close the Gap. From 2013 to 2017, we've seen social media users turn to Twitter for news at an alarming rate—a spike from 52 percent to 74 percent—with Facebook climbing at a similar rate, from 47

We want certainty against our best interests.

percent to 68 percent.[56] Sure, Twitter and Facebook are an easy way for us to close that cognitive loop. But they are also riddled with poor information, limited source credibility, and no checks on validity. Damn it, I guess I have to say it: they're riddled with "fake news." A problem for even traditional news, never mind unregulated social media.[57]

One might suggest the US is experiencing turbulent times. Sadly, this assertion only deepens our reliance on social media for news, as both usage evidence suggests and Kruglanski and Webster's findings show that NFC rises with crisis. This dire need for certainty might be just another great explanation for the Outcome Fallacy. Valuing outcomes over processes is an easier, quicker, and more comfortable way for us to satisfy our NFC. Or, as Jerome Kagan has pointed out, certainty is motivating us.

DISSONANCE: *A lack of harmony between online and offline behavior.*

Have you ever thought, "This person is nothing like how they present themselves online?" Or maybe, "I wish the world knew what this person was really like?" They're kind of crappy things to think, but I'm pretty sure we've all been there. Why does this lack of harmony even matter?

Dan Ariely, a behavioral economics professor at Duke University, has conducted some insightful research on dishonesty.[58] Two of his findings seem to provide more insight than any others. First, the further you remove someone from the act of deceit, the more capable they are of being deceitful. Second, people are more susceptible to lying if it stays within boundaries where they can still feel good about themselves. The online environment seems like the perfect setting for the deceitful. The overly certain.

People appear to be more susceptible to cheating, lying, or embellishing online. Why? They're further removed from communication, and this decreases the pain associated with being deceitful. All while providing a safe zone for people to still feel good about themselves. I mean, *everyone else is doing it.* So while we might end up going to social media to quickly close that cognitive loop, it's more than likely you could experience adverse effects. In the end, dissonance creates a magnifying effect on "digital" certainty. A breeding ground for the charlatans, fakes, and frauds. An online environment where you'll probably wind up frustrated, annoyed, and perhaps even more confused. In 2019, dare I say it? Maybe we should be spending a little more time face to face.

The problem with all of this certainty is simple. The world is uncertain. Most things are quite uncertain. You'll never know if that product is any good until you buy it. You won't know what that entrepreneurial endeavor provides unless you do it. You won't know life with someone else unless you break up with your current partner. You won't be able to close the Gap unless you go deeper than 280 characters.

Our systemic need for certainty is just *more* counterforce on closing the Gap. There's a question I sometimes get from people in transition: "Doug, you seem passionate. How do you find your passion?" I respond, "Just start doing stuff. Namely stuff you like." Typically, they look underwhelmed, having expected some grander response. It's a look that's screaming for certainty in an uncertain world. Most things cannot be folded up, boxed in, and figured out. Randomness assures us of that.

An uncertain state is necessary to navigate the Gap. A state of ongoing curiosity. A state that knows that almost nothing is absolute. A state where status and dominance don't rule our behavior, without that arrogance that demands us to stubbornly insist, "I know." It's easier to wilt to this ugly side of ego than it is to remain uncertain. We've inherited it from our ancestors. It's how we've been wired. It's what we know. It's more comfortable.

My advice is to question the overly certain specialists and gatekeepers. What is the downside? What are my possible negative outcomes? If they can't answer these questions, either they haven't thought about it or they're lying to you. In either case, run. Run fast, looking for someone who can give you the downside. You're in search of specialists and gatekeepers using well-thought-through logic, reason, or data to support their level of certainty. You need someone willing to embrace uncertainty with you. There's typically a downside, and there are *always* problems. I'm *fairly certain*, anyway.

PROBLEMS

"There are no solutions. There are only trade-offs."

Thomas Sowell

In 1980, Mothers Against Drunk Driving (MADD) was founded. They lobbied to alter drinking laws and deservingly stigmatized drunk driving. Pop culture took notice and got behind MADD's message full force. Car companies started making cars safer, laws stiffened, and awareness rose. If car crash death rates had remained the same as in 1980, approximately 650,000 more people in America would have died in car crashes today. That deaths haven't risen is even more stunning, considering that in 1980, Americans drove 1.5 trillion miles, compared to 2013, where they doubled it to 3 trillion.[59] A testament to progress in road safety. We think, "Finally, the roads are safe."

Well, not so fast. Distracted driving remains a huge problem. Death reduction is great, but we also need accident reduction. The focus has moved away from booze and on to the mobile phone. Its usage while driving is a problem. As of 2014, one of every four car crashes involved cell phone use.[60] Now, we see signs posted on highways reading "Do Not Text and Drive," police do road stops in our communities, and cell phone fines have been raised. Prevention of distracted driving has clearly become a point of focus. I'm willing to bet on our ability to improve this issue long term, just like we did with drunk driving.

What does this have to do with the Gap?

I used to fall victim to Grass Is Always Greener Syndrome, until I realized new grass just means new problems. Despite what every politician wants to tell you, there will likely never be a cure-all. It's a pipe dream as far-fetched as the one where I get my dad to stop yelling at the TV. I believe in progress, and I believe we've made tremendous progress in many areas. More than anything, I believe every decision, choice, or action brings with it another set of problems. Problems don't go away; problems change. Just another reason why you should only trust specialists who account for the downside.

Would you suggest not inventing the mobile phone just to stymie the distracted driving problem? That sounds ludicrous, doesn't it. Especially considering the safety mobile phones have *added* to society. You literally now have a lifeline with you twenty-four hours a day. Think of all the untabulated lives cell phones have saved. Text messages sent in emergencies. Calls made to say, "Don't worry honey, I'm on my way home."

Problems don't go away; problems change.

SCALE: *A variable worth considering.*

Let's assume you're an astronaut. Would a power outage in your spaceship during space travel be the same as a power outage in your home during a storm? In both cases, we have the same issue: a power outage. But one problem is clearly more drastic than the other. A power outage at home might be temporarily inconvenient. A power outage in space might mean death. Problems have an element of scale. A brake rotor problem on a BMW costs more to fix than one on a Honda. A roof on a 3,000 square-foot house costs more than one on a 1,000 square-foot house. A culture problem in a five-person business is easier to fix than in a five-hundred-person business.

We often assume money solves problems. I guess it's possible. Depending on your problem. Typically, money just magnifies the element of scale associated with problems. It's a derivative of the Outcome Fallacy. Maybe that's why Bernie Madoff orchestrated a $65 billion Ponzi scheme.[62] One might point to greed. That would be plausible. I'd say it's a matter of a problem scaling. When you're robbing Peter to pay Paul, this only escalates the overall problem with each higher dollar amount stolen. I'm not suggesting you feel bad for Madoff. I'm saying problems have scalability.

Uber was founded in 2009, and ten years later, they have a potential market cap of $120 billion.[61] Why? They've solved lots of problems. They transport drunk drivers. This aided in that decline of car crash deaths. They have user profiles and track rides. This makes transportation safer and more reliable. They use on-demand rider-driver matching, which saves people tons of time. They've scaled internationally, which eliminates language barriers and makes travel easier. They even have this unexplainable factor that has made taking Ubers cool, which has helped out both parents and teens everywhere. That aspect alone is pretty amazing, when you think about it.

My first night on vacation in San Juan, I requested an Uber to take me to dinner. The driver insisted on picking me up down the street from the hotel. When I got in the car, I asked him why. He told me, "Uber drivers can't be seen by taxi owners." I said, "Wow, that bad, huh?" He looked back at me and said, "So bad, they start fights and vandalize cars." It didn't take long before I saw just how bad. Later that weekend, I witnessed an irate taxi driver smash the hood of an Uber car. I thought to myself, "This is a problem." Taxis are being replaced, people are losing their jobs, and violence has ensued. Uber has created these problems. Since Uber is everywhere, these problems have scaled. Does that mean Uber shouldn't have been created?

I'll leave you to evaluate the trade-off. That's what is required of Gap closers. The Outcome Fallacy reminds us there will never be one singular outcome that exonerates you from all problems. Problems will be plentiful. Problems are inevitable. Problems never go away; they just change. It's a Gap navigation best practice to evaluate trade-offs. What problems do you want? What problems don't you want? What solutions do you value more? Most? Or, not at all? What is the trade-off?

Of course, all *these* transportation problems I described above will just change again with the onset of self-driving cars and the imminent all-around automation of society. This will present big problems. Big problems that provide big opportunities. Of course, this will depend on what side of the coin you're looking at. Do you consider problems to be opportunities or just problems? I am proposing you adopt a new three-part mindset toward problems: 1) they never go away; they just change, 2) they have an element of scale, and 3) they present opportunities. This mindset will make it significantly easier for you to navigate whatever Gap you're trying to close.

NAIVETÉ

"More is lost by indecision than wrong
decision. Indecision is the thief of opportunity.
It will steal you blind."

Cicero

In 1945, a young man named Samuel found a Ben Franklin variety store for sale in Newport, Arkansas. It was listed for $25,000. The problem was he was nothing more than a bright-eyed twenty-seven-year-old with an inkling for retail and $5,000 in his pocket. He had no experience running a store, negotiating contracts, or doing pretty much anything required of a business owner. Fortunately, he was able to scrounge up the additional $20,000. He signed the purchase contract and jumped right in.

He quickly realized the previous owners had been trying to offload this store for a while. It was only doing $72,000 a year, much of which went to expenses. But he was determined to make it work. He tried everything. He even teetered on breaking Ben Franklin's franchise rules. He drove state to state to get better wholesale prices on items instead of buying them from Ben Franklin corporate wholesalers. He found loopholes to make it work. He bought popcorn machines and ice cream makers to draw in customers. He heard a competitor across the street was going to expand into a neighboring department store, so he beat him to the punch. He bought the department store and named it the Eagle Store. He was now running two stores and business was good. Sure, he was busy, but within five years, he'd grown that Ben Franklin into the biggest variety store in Arkansas, pulling in $250,000. Everything was going great.

Until it was time to renew his lease. Five years earlier, Samuel hadn't included an option to renew in the contract. He didn't know any better at the time. His landlord decided not to renew the lease, wanting to secure it for his son. He knew Samuel had no other options. His strategy was to push Samuel out. Samuel was heartbroken. He and his wife had built a life in Newport. They were just settling into their new home with four children. It was truly a nightmare situation.

Ultimately, Samuel decided to sell the Eagle Store and all its goods to the competitor across the street and let him expand. Instead of feeling sorry for himself, he gathered his thoughts, picked everything up, and started all over again. It was time to look for a new store in a new town.

He ended up finding that new location in Bentonville, Arkansas. This would be the start of Sam Walton's legendary retail empire, Walmart. In Walton's autobiography, he writes, "The whole thing was probably a blessing. I had a chance for a brand-new start, and this time I knew what I was doing."[63] Time and time again, this ends up being the story. Early failures and experiences teach us the lessons we need to succeed in the future. Walton admits many of the philosophies that would make Walmart, Walmart, stemmed from things he did in that Newport variety store. Bud Walton, Sam's brother who worked alongside him, said:

> The Newport store was really the beginning of where Walmart is today. We did everything. We would wash windows, sweep floors, trim windows. We did all the stockroom work, checked the freight in. Everything it took to run a store. We had to keep expenses at a minimum. That's where it started, years ago. Our money was made by controlling expenses. That, and Sam always being ingenious. He never stopped trying to do something different.

Walton embraced his own naiveté to succeed. He invested in his future with action. He didn't let problems, like the fact he didn't know anything about contracts or negotiations, stop him. He just kept moving and learning along the way, knowing every attempt to close the Gap would yield more insight and revelations. He realized sometimes you need to lose to win.

There's no way around it: if you want to close the Gap, you have to embrace the fact you don't have the wisdom, experience, or skills to succeed yet. You don't know what you don't know. You're *not* stupid. There's a vast difference between

Invest in stupidity now for wisdom later.

looking stupid and being stupid. You have to be willing to *look* stupid. That's smart. You're making an investment in your future self. Invest in stupidity now for wisdom later. There's a good chance you'll have to make another adjustment in the future. Just like Walmart has to adjust with the onslaught that Amazon and other online retailers brought. They have to reinvest in stupidity. They have to embrace their own naiveté again. Will they? I don't know. But they have to. Just like you and I do. This cycle never ends. The Gap persists.

FINAL WORDS

"I wish that I were good
No man, I wish that I were great
And I wish that I'd been early
More often than late
But nothing lasts forever
Maybe that's fate"

Langhorne Slim

In my early teen years, I volunteered at an Alzheimer's home. It's really sad to see an incurable disease take over someone's mind. Alzheimer's slowly destroys memory and other mental functions. Ultimately ending in demise. I remember very few things from that experience. I remember feeling bad for the residents. I remember having to reintroduce myself to residents each time I visited. I remember one patient named Yolanda. We'd play board games together. She made me laugh and smile every time we interacted. She was full of wit, spunk, and joy.

One day, I showed up and asked the nurse to see Yolanda. She told me, "Doug, Yolanda's not with us anymore." I'd like to say that was some massive turning point in my life. An eye-opener, or something that taught me a grand lesson. I was shocked, but unscathed at the time. Too young to really make sense of it. I've done too many stupid things in my life that would contradict suggesting I'd experienced any major epiphany at age thirteen. Today, I think about Yolanda from time to time. Although it's a scattered memory, it serves as a reality check. A reminder that life slows down for nobody. What's here today could be gone tomorrow. The regrets I'll have when it's my turn to go will be the things I was close-minded about. And it probably won't have been too hard to be that way, considering our innate motivation toward close-mindedness. I'm determined to push back on counterforce and to look at both sides of the coin. I'm determined to be guided by curiosity and to not allow herd mentality to dictate my direction. I'm determined to be more open-minded. Will you join me? Maybe these parting words will help.

In the heart of Tualatin Valley sits Beaverton, Oregon. It's just west of Portland, at the base of the snow-capped Mount Hood. Approximately 89,000 residents call it home. In 1964, two of those residents, Bill Bowerman and Phil Knight, founded one of the most successful companies of the twenty-first century: a sportswear company called Blue Ribbon Sports. It wasn't until 1978 that this company became the recognizable behemoth we know today, when it was renamed Nike.

In 1988, Wieden+Kennedy was the ad agency responsible for Nike's first big television advertising push. In a 2009 *AdWeek* interview, co-founder Dan Wieden was asked about how that campaign came together. He remembered being worried the night before presenting the finished product to Nike. He thought the eight spots in the $25 million campaign lacked cohesiveness. Until he came upon this epiphany:

> For some damn reason, I thought of Gary Gilmore, who actually grew up in Portland…Gary had killed some people in Utah, which is not a good place to kill people because they kill you right back. So, he was convicted and sentenced to die by firing squad. A little old fashioned, but they brought him out, put him in the chair, and the firing squad was there. Before they put the sack over his head, they asked him if he had any last words. And he said, "Let's do it."[64]

Wieden dropped the "let's." Nike's legendary "Just Do It" slogan was born. Wieden recollected how amazed he was that when Gary Gilmore was in the face of uncertainty, it was those three words that pushed him through that moment. Wieden went on to say, "The history of the line 'Just Do It' is probably a good peek into the unconscious and where ideas come from. And why nobody knows."

"Just Do It" might be the greatest slogan of all time. The simplicity and pertinence for almost every situation in life is undeniable. It applies to you as you look to close whatever Gap you're looking to close. You just have to go for it.

MORTALITY: *A good starting point for navigating the Gap.*

One day, you're going to die. And I mean that quite literally. One day, undoubtedly, you will be dead. I wish there was more to conclude here, but there just isn't. It's a fact.

The thought of your beatless heart, brittle bones, and cold decaying body might seem morbid. Unhealthy, to a degree. I will try to convince you otherwise. Maybe we don't want to face the truth. That one day we'll leave behind our loved ones. We'll no longer be able to see our children play tee-ball, smile at our spouses across the dinner table, or hear our friends on the other end of the phone. One day, it will be over. That *all* seems scary as hell.

In between the day you're born and the day you die, pretty much anything is possible. We may waste time in the same crappy situation, join communities that hold us down, or expend energy telling the world how bad we've got it. I assure you, none of these situations are permanent. In this life, *nothing* is off the table. Death is undeniably true, and it forces us to come to grips with reality.

It demands you take a step back and understand the realness of everything around you. Do you like what you know? Do you like what you do? Do you like who you are with? All of these questions start to ring in your ears. They become as real as the reality you observe before you. You're facing your death. In doing so, it screams to you, "You will die. And when you do, there will be more you don't know than you do know. So go now, hurry up, explore, and start to close the Gap."

I'm quite aware that what I'm asking you to do is not easy. In fact, most of the time what is simple is not easy. Although we have a tendency to confuse the two. Our ego tricks us, we believe simplicity is too easy, and we protect that ego by making things sound more complex. Or possibly it's our laziness that tells us simplicity is actually hard. As I've documented, we have an aversion toward being uncomfortable. In the end, we decide it's easier to just stay put. If we're going to close the Gap, we need to embrace simplicity. Simplicity is the secret to reproducibility, engagement, and performance. It will help you stay the course.

Steve Jobs once said, "Simple can be harder than complex: You have to work hard to get your thinking clean to make it simple. But it's worth it in the end because once you get there, you can move mountains." Maybe that's why his iPhone has an addictive-like quality to it. A design so simple it can move mountains. It's a model for every piece of technology that followed. In modern times, simplicity has become a prerequisite for sustainability. Be the judge of that statement. Consumers won't tolerate complexity. You'll often find that simplicity is at the heart of everything great. That's how you're going to close the Gap. Simplicity compounded over time.

It wasn't easy for Kobe Bryant to adopt an insane training schedule. But it was simple. Wake up earlier and train more. It wasn't easy for the Rolling Stones to write their first song. But it was simple. According to Keith Richards, they just needed to be locked in a kitchen by their manager.[65] It wasn't easy for comedians to strike it big in 1970. But it was simple. Stay up late at night, play at big city open mics and comedy clubs, and wait to get picked. This is precisely why I think Nike got it right. Everything typically boils down to those three simple words: Just Do It. Sam Walton clearly embodied that slogan as he embraced naiveté. You'll have to as well in order to close the Gap. In case you need me to jog your memory. Here's a simple checklist to guide you:

- ✓ Recognize the Gap.
- ✓ Value quality over quantity.
- ✓ Face the enemies in your life.
- ✓ Evaluate people's worldviews.
- ✓ Push back on counterforce.
- ✓ Embrace the unknown.
- ✓ Identify gatekeepers in your life.
- ✓ Use access to your advantage.
- ✓ Rely on specialists (but not too much).
- ✓ Don't stumble on contradiction.
- ✓ Watch out for private interests.
- ✓ Be aware of human bias.
- ✓ Consider the entertainment factor.

- ✓ Weigh the elements of pressure.
- ✓ Don't let your intelligence drown you.
- ✓ Never stop asking questions.
- ✓ Say no to lumping.
- ✓ Place high value on the process.
- ✓ Account for randomness.
- ✓ Look at the entire picture.
- ✓ Model the right people, places, and things.
- ✓ Embrace uncertainty.
- ✓ Challenge too much certainty.
- ✓ Adopt a new mindset toward problems.
- ✓ Assess the trade-offs.
- ✓ Be willing to look stupid.
- ✓ Leverage mortality.
- ✓ Keep it simple and compound it.
- ✓ Be more open-minded.

Our problem is the Gap, that little space between what you know and don't know. Closing it won't be easy. It's going to take consistency and commitment. Especially as you start to learn more and grow more. While I'd love for you to scream from the mountaintops in support of open-mindedness, I'd be just as honored if you tapped your neighbor on the shoulder and whispered it in their ear. It's often said the first step on a million-mile journey is the hardest. I've hopefully empowered you to take the first step. At the very least, challenged you to look at the world a little differently.

You're left with a mere decision, for which I really only see three options:

1. You can fold your hand. You pitch a tent and never approach the Gap. You're okay with what you know, what you've done, and what you've experienced. Some might call this a life of ignorance. A life adrift, while the world tosses you every which way. Oblivious, maybe. Content, probably.

2. You can dig in your heels and defend your ground. A life dedicated to motivated close-mindedness. Not willing to budge. Not willing to venture across the Gap in fear of what your tribe might think or what you might find out. You see no advantage in doing so. You're totally committed to your current beliefs at all costs.

3. You can try to close the Gap. You choose a life of exploration. Not necessarily in the physical sense of the word, but it could be. You explore ideas, beliefs, and concepts. You choose curiosity. You let yourself be challenged by the thrill of what you might find out. You stand up for what you believe, but you also allow yourself to be inspired by anything and anyone. You're completely aware of that little space between what you know and what you don't know.

Which will you choose?

ACKNOWLEDGMENTS

I do something a little strange when I read a book. I usually read the acknowledgments before I start. I guess it helps me build empathy for the author. Just in case I don't like or I disagree with the book, it reminds me the author is human. It might even help me understand their worldview a little bit better. You probably didn't do that with this book, but that's okay. I'm not sharing too much here anyway. But hey, maybe you'll start in the future.

To you, the reader. This book is for you. It's meaningless without you. Ideas are powerless in the hands and minds of no one. For any idea to spread, it needs believers, advocates, and champions. I hope you are one for the Gap.

To my amazing editor, Chantel Hamilton. You've been more like a writing coach for me. My appreciation runs incredibly deep for your guidance and support. This book would not have been possible without you.

To all the writers, artists, and creatives who have inspired my worldview. In many ways, this book is just an iteration on your work. When we meet, if we meet, I will happily share this with you in person.

To my family and friends who support me in all my

endeavors. That support means everything to me.

To my extensive team at Amplify Publishing who helped me bring this book to life. You are all rockstars.

Thank you.

NOTES

INTRODUCTION

1. Fred Shapiro, "Quotes Uncovered: Death and Taxes," *Freakonomics*, February 17, 2011, http://freakonomics.com/2011/02/17/quotes-uncovered-death-and-taxes.
2. Bella DePaulo, "What Is the Divorce Rate, Really?," *Psychology Today*, February 2, 2017, https://www.psychologytoday.com/us/blog/living-single/201702/what-is-the-divorce-rate-really.
3. "The Whys and Hows of Generations Research," *Pew Research Center*, September 3, 2015, http://www.people-press.org/2015/09/03/the-whys-and-hows-of-generations-research.

WORLDVIEWS

4. Laura Krantz, "'Bell Curve' Author Attacked by Protesters at Middlebury College," *Boston Globe*, March 5, 2017, https://www.bostonglobe.com/metro/2017/03/04/middlebury/hAfpA1Hquh7DIS1doiKbhJ/story.html.
5. Sam Harris, "#73 - Forbidden Knowledge: A Conversation with Charles Murray," *Waking Up*, audio, 2:18:01, https://samharris.org/podcasts/forbidden-knowledge.
6. Ezra Klein, "The Sam Harris Debate," *Vox*, April 9, 2018, https://www.vox.com/2018/4/9/17210248/sam-harris-ezra-klein-charles-murray-transcript-podcast.
7. Ray Dalio, "The Key to Bridgewater's Success: A Real Idea

Meritocracy," *LinkedIn*, September 23, 2107, https://www.linkedin.com/pulse/key-bridgewaters-success-real-idea-meritocracy-ray-dalio

8. Andrew Gelman, "The Twentieth-Century Reversal: How Did the Republican States Switch to the Democrats and Vice Versa?," *Statistics and Public Policy* 1, no. 1 (2014): http://www.stat.columbia.edu/~gelman/research/published/reversal2.pdf; and Natalie Wolchover, "Why Did the Democrats and Republicans Switch Platforms?," *Live Science*, September 24, 2012, https://www.livescience.com/34241-democratic-republican-parties-switch-platforms.html.

9. "List of Presidents of the United States," *Wikipedia*, last modified October 23, 2018, https://en.wikipedia.org/wiki/List_of_Presidents_of_the_United_States

10. Conrad Hackett and David McClendon, "Christians Remain World's Largest Religious Group, but They Are Declining in Europe," Pew Research, April 5, 2017, http://www.pewresearch.org/fact-tank/2017/04/05/christians-remain-worlds-largest-religious-group-but-they-are-declining-in-europe.

11. "Music," The Rolling Stones Official Website, http://www.rollingstones.com/release/aftermath-uk/ and "The Rolling Stones," *Wikipedia*, last modified October 23, 2018, https://en.wikipedia.org/wiki/The_Rolling_Stones.

MATCHING

12. "How Uber Works," Uber, https://www.uber.com/about/how-does-uber-work.

13. Tyler Cowen, *The Complacent Class: The Self-Defeating Quest for the American Dream* (New York: St. Martin's, 2017), 15.

14. Tim Soulo, "91% of Content Gets No Traffic From Google. And How to Be in the Other 9%," *Ahrefs Blog*, May 31, 2018, https://

ahrefs.com/blog/search-traffic-study.

15. Douglas Vigliotti, *The Salesperson Paradox* (2018), 179.

UNKNOWN

16. Maury Brown, "A Look Back on the First ABC Monday Night Football on Its 45th Anniversary," *Forbes*, September 21, 2015, https://www.forbes.com/sites/maurybrown/2015/09/21/a-look-back-on-the-first-abc-monday-night-football-on-its-45th-anniversary.

17. Richard Sandomir, "ESPN Pays Top Dollar for Football, but Audience Isn't Buying," *New York Times*, November 28, 2016, https://www.nytimes.com/2016/11/28/sports/football/monday-night-football-tv-ratings-espn.html.

18. Will Brinson, "Fox Sports Gives NFL $3.3 Billion for 'Thursday Night Football' Package over Five Years," CBS Sports, January 31, 2018, https://www.cbssports.com/nfl/news/fox-sports-gives-nfl-3-3-billion-for-thursday-night-football-package-over-five-years.

GATEKEEPERS

19. "14 A-Listers Who Got Their Start on The Tonight Show," *TV Guide*, https://www.tvguide.com/galleries/tonight-show-johnny-carson-debuts-comedians.

20. Brian Lowry, "'I'm Dying' Crowns Johnny Carson as Comedy King-maker," CNN, June 2, 2017, https://www.cnn.com/2017/06/02/entertainment/johnny-carson-im-dying-up-here/index.html.

21. Joe Rhodes, "Carson's Code," *New York Times*, January 30, 2005, https://www.nytimes.com/2005/01/30/arts/television/carsons-code.html.

22. Mitchell Stevens, "History of Television," *Grolier Encyclopedia*, https://www.nyu.edu/classes/stephens/History%20of%20Television%20page.htm.

SPECIALISTS

23. "Halo Effect," *Wikipedia*, last modified October 22, 2018, https://en.wikipedia.org/wiki/Halo_effect.

24. Gregory Wallace, "Voter Turnout at 20-year Low in 2016," CNN, November 30, 2016, https://www.cnn.com/2016/11/11/politics/popular-vote-turnout-2016/index.html; Christopher Ingraham, "About 100 Million People Couldn't Be Bothered to Vote This Year," *Washington Post*, November 12, 2016, https://www.washingtonpost.com/news/wonk/wp/2016/11/12/about-100-million-people-couldnt-be-bothered-to-vote-this-year; "Voter Turnout in Presidential Elections," American Presidency Project, http://www.presidency.ucsb.edu/data/turnout.php; "Estimates of the Voting Age Population for 2016," and *Federal Register*, January 30, 2017, https://www.federalregister.gov/documents/2017/01/30/2017-01890/estimates-of-the-voting-age-population-for-2016.

INTEREST

25. Paul Farhi, "Washington Post Closes Sale to Amazon Founder Jeff Bezos," *Washington Post*, October 1, 2013, https://www.washingtonpost.com/business/economy/washington-post-closes-sale-to-amazon-founder-jeff-bezos/2013/10/01/fca3b16a-2acf-11e3-97a3-ff2758228523_story.html.

26. "Marc Benioff is the Latest Tech Billionaire to Buy a Famous Magazine," *Economist*, September 20, 2018, https://www.economist.com/business/2018/09/22/marc-benioff-is-the-latest-tech-billionaire-to-buy-a-famous-magazine.

27. Ryan Gaydos, "Kanye West's 'Ye' Hits No. 1 on Billboard Chart Following Pro-Trump Rants," Fox News, June 13, 2018, http://www.foxnews.com/entertainment/2018/06/13/kanye-wests-ye-hits-no-1-on-billboard-chart-following-pro-trump-rants.html.

28. "Joe Rogan Experience #1169 - Elon Musk," YouTube video, 2:37:02, posted by PowerfulJRE, September 6, 2018, https://www.youtube.com/watch?v=ycPr5-27vSI.

BIAS

29. Jeff Desjardins, "Every Single Cognitive Bias in One Infographic," *Visual Capitalist*, September 25, 2017, http://www.visualcapitalist.com/every-single-cognitive-bias.

30. Daniel Kahneman, "Prospect Theory", in *Thinking, Fast and Slow* (New York: Farrar, Straus and Giroux, 2011), 278–88.

ENTERTAINMENT

31. "Howard Stern," Biography, https://www.biography.com/people/howard-stern-9494041.

32. Bill Carter and Christine Hauser, "Howard Stern to Shift Show to Satellite Radio in 2006," *New York Times*, October 6, 2004, https://www.nytimes.com/2004/10/06/business/media/howard-stern-to-shift-show-to-satellite-radio-in-2006.html.

33. Ben Sisario, "Howard Stern and SiriusXM Sign New Deal for 5 Years," *New York Times*, December 15, 2015, https://www.nytimes.com/2015/12/16/business/media/howard-stern-and-siriusxm-reach-new-deal.html.

34. Howard Stern, on *My Next Guest Needs No Introduction with David Letterman*, episode 6, "Howard Stern," released May 31, 2018, on Netflix.

35. Jonah Berger, *Contagious: Why Things Catch On* (New York: Simon & Schuster, 2013), 24.

36. Jim Chairusmi, "When Super Bowl Scoring Peaks—or Timing Your Bathroom Break," *Wall Street Journal*, February 4, 2017, https://www.wsj.com/articles/when-super-bowl-scoring-peaksor-timing-your-bathroom-break-1486117801.

INTELLIGENCE

37. Chip Heath and Dan Heath, "The Curse of Knowledge," *Harvard Business Review*, December 2006, https://hbr.org/2006/12/the-curse-of-knowledge

38. "The Brain That Changes Itself," YouTube video, 51:51, posted by Over the Horizon, May 26, 2013, https://www.youtube.com/watch?v=bFCOm1P_cQQ.

39. "Kids Ask About 73 Questions A Day, Many Parents Can't Answer," CBS Boston, December 11, 2017, http://boston.cbslocal.com/2017/12/11/kids-73-questions-each-day.

LUMPING

40. "Timeline: America's War on Drugs," April 2, 2007, NPR, https://www.npr.org/templates/story/story.php?storyId=9252490.

41. Robert Hornik et al., "Effects of the National Youth Anti-Drug Media Campaign on Youths," *American Journal of Public Health* 98, no. 12 (December 2008): https://www.ncbi.nlm.nih.gov/pmc/articles/PMC2636541.

42. Berger, *Contagious*, 151.

43. Michael Pollan, *How to Change Your Mind: What the New Science of Psychedelics Teaches Us About Consciousness, Dying, Addiction, Depression, and Transcendence* (New York: Penguin, 2018).

OUTCOMES

44. "Kobe Bryant," Basketball Reference, https://www.basketball-reference.com/players/b/bryanko01.html.

45. Kobe Bryant, "TEDxShanghaiSalon: Power of the Mind," YouTube video, 42:06, posted by Richard Hsu, July 25, 2016, https://youtu.be/9_tYXFbgjZk.

46. Kobe Bryant, "Dear Basketball," *Players' Tribune*, November 29,

2015, https://www.theplayerstribune.com/en-us/articles/dear-basketball.

47. Douglas Vigliotti, "The Outcome Fallacy," *#DVBlog*, April 10, 2018, http://douglasvigliotti.com/blog/the-outcome-fallacy.

RANDOMNESS

48. "What Is Chaos Theory?," FractalFoundation.org, https://fractalfoundation.org/resources/what-is-chaos-theory.

49. Annie Duke, *Thinking in Bets: Making Smarter Decisions When You Don't Have All the Facts* (New York: Portfolio/Penguin, 2018).

50. Stephanie Vozza, "The Random Events That Sparked 8 of the World's Biggest Startups," *Fast Company*, November 3, 2014, Fast Company https://www.fastcompany.com/3037896/the-random-events-that-sparked-8-of-the-worlds-biggest-startups.

CERTAINTY

51. J. Kagan, "Motives and Development," *Journal of Personality and Social Psychology* 22, no. 1 (1972): 51–66.

52. Maria Konnikova, "Why We Need Answers," *New Yorker*, April 30, 2013, https://www.newyorker.com/tech/annals-of-technology/why-we-need-answers.

53. D. M. Webster and A. W. Kruglanski, "Individual Differences in Need for Cognitive Closure," *Journal of Personality and Social Psychology*, no. 67 (1994): 1049–62.

54. Arie W. Kruglanski, "The Need for Closure: Motivated Closed Mindedness," TerpConnect, 2012, http://terpconnect.umd.edu/~hannahk/The_Need_for_Closure.html.

55. A. W. Kruglanski and D. M. Webster, D. M. "Motivated Closing of the Mind: 'Seizing' and 'Freezing,'" *Psychological Review*, no. 103 (1996): 263–83.

56. Elisa Shearer and Jeffrey Gottfried, "News Use across Social

Media Platforms 2017," Pew Research Center, September 7, 2017, http://www.journalism.org/2017/09/07/news-use-across-social-media-platforms-2017

57. "Fake News, Lies and Propaganda: How to Sort Fact from Fiction," University of Michigan Library, Research Guides, last updated August 17, 2018, http://guides.lib.umich.edu/c.php?g=637508&p=4462356.

58. Dan Ariely, in *(Dis)Honesty: The Truth About Lies*, directed by Yael Melamede (US: Salty Features, 2015).

PROBLEMS

59. Steven Pinker, *Enlightenment Now: The Case for Reason, Science, Humanism, and Progress* (New York: Viking, 2018), 177, 178.

60. "Texting & Driving," DMV.org, October 26, 2018, https://www.dmv.org/distracted-driving/texting-and-driving.php.

61. Liz Hoffman, Greg Bensinger, and Maureen Farrell, "Uber Proposals Value Company at $120 Billion in a Possible IPO," *The Wall Street Journal*, October 16, 2018, https://www.wsj.com/articles/uber-proposals-value-company-at-120-billion-in-a-possible-ipo-1539690343.

62. "Bernard Madoff," Biography, https://www.biography.com/people/bernard-madoff-466366.

NAVIETÉ

63. Sam Walton with John Huey, *Sam Walton: Made in America* (New York, Bantam, 2012), 40.

FINAL WORDS

64. Dan Wieden, "Dan Wieden on Just Do It," YouTube video, 3:00, posted by blogestalo, November 16, 2009, https://youtu.

be/kr9tNQr6VRM.

65. Keith Richards, "Online Exclusive: Keith Richards Uncut," interview by David Fricke, *Rolling Stone*, September 24, 2002, https://www.rollingstone.com/music/news/online-exclusive-keith-richards-uncut-20020924.

MORE TO HELP YOU CLOSE THE GAP

Sign up for my private reading list at DVReadingList.com

I write a private reading list every month to help people build a reading habit. I'm a big believer in continuous learning and self-education. I read about 50-60 books a year (mostly non-fiction.) Each month I write one email with three book recommendations. I share my favorite quote from the book, give a brief overview, and provide my immediate takeaways. As a subscriber you'll also get my newest articles and podcast episodes as they're published.

Invite me to speak on *The Gap* by emailing speak@ douglasvigliotti.com

One of the best ways to fully grasp ideas is through discussion and hearing them presented live. I've designed a book talk to provide a deeper level of meaning to *The Gap*. For more details, just email the address above.

Visit my website at DouglasVigliotti.com

Here's where you'll be able to find out more about me, get in contact with me, and engage with some of my content. I publish new articles and podcast episodes regularly on my website.